ART BOOKS

FROM CRESCENT MOON PUBLISHING

Leonardo da Vinci
by James Pearson

Early Netherlandish Painting
by Rosalind Mutter

Piero della Francesca
by Naomi Haskell

Giovanni Bellini
by Julia Davis

Eric Gill: Nuptials of God
by Anthony Hoyland

Minimal Art and Artists In the 1960s and After
by Laura Garrard

Postwar Art
by George Knighton

Vincent van Gogh: Visionary Landscapes
by Stuart Morris

Max Beckmann
by Stuart Morris

Egon Schiele: Sex and Death in Purple Stockings
by D. Simon Eade

Mark Rothko: The Art of Transcendence
by Julia Davis

Jasper Johns
by L.M. Poole

Brice Marden
by Laura Garrard

Frank Stella: American Abstract Artist
by James Pearson

The Light Eternal: J.M.W. Turner
by Jeremy Mark Robinson

Maurice Sendak and the Art of Children's Book Illustration
by L.M. Poole

Sex in Art: Pornography and Pleasure in Painting and Sculpture
by Cassidy Hughes

Glorification: Religious Abstraction
In Renaissance and 20th Century Painting
by Jeremy Mark Robinson

The Art of Andy Goldsworthy
by William Malpas

Andy Goldsworthy: Touching Nature
by William Malpas

Andy Goldsworthy In Close-Up
by William Malpas

The Art of Richard Long
by William Malpas

Constantin Brancusi: Sculpting the Essence of Things
by James Pearson

Alison Wilding: The Embrace of Sculpture
by Susan Quinnell

The Erotic Object: Sexuality in Sculpture
From Prehistory to the Present Day
by Susan Quinnell

Land Art: A Complete Guide to Landscape, Environmental,
Earthworks, Nature, Sculpture and Installation Art
by William Malpas

Land Art In Close-Up
by William Malpas

Colourfield Painting: Minimal, Cool, Hard Edge, Serial
and Post-Painterly Abstract Art From the Sixties to the Present
by Laura Garrard

PERUGINO

PERUGINO

GEORGE C. WILLIAMSON, LITT.D.

AUTHOR OF
"JOHN RUSSELL, R.A.," "RICHARD COSWAY, R.A., AND HIS
WIFE AND PUPILS," "PORTRAIT MINIATURES,"
"BERNARDINO LUINI," ETC.

CRESCENT MOON

First published 1903. This edition © 2017.

Printed and bound in the U.S.A.
Set in Book Antiqua 10 on 14pt.
Designed by Radiance Graphics.

Thanks to the authors and publishers quoted.

British Library Cataloguing in Publication data

ISBN-13 9781861716066 (Pbk)
ISBN-13 9781861717030 (Hbk)

CRESCENT MOON PUBLISHING
P.O. Box 1312, Maidstone, Kent, ME14 5XU
Great Britain, www.crmoon.com

CONTENTS

NOTE ON THE TEXT

The text is from *Perugino* by George Williamson, published by G. Bell, 1903.

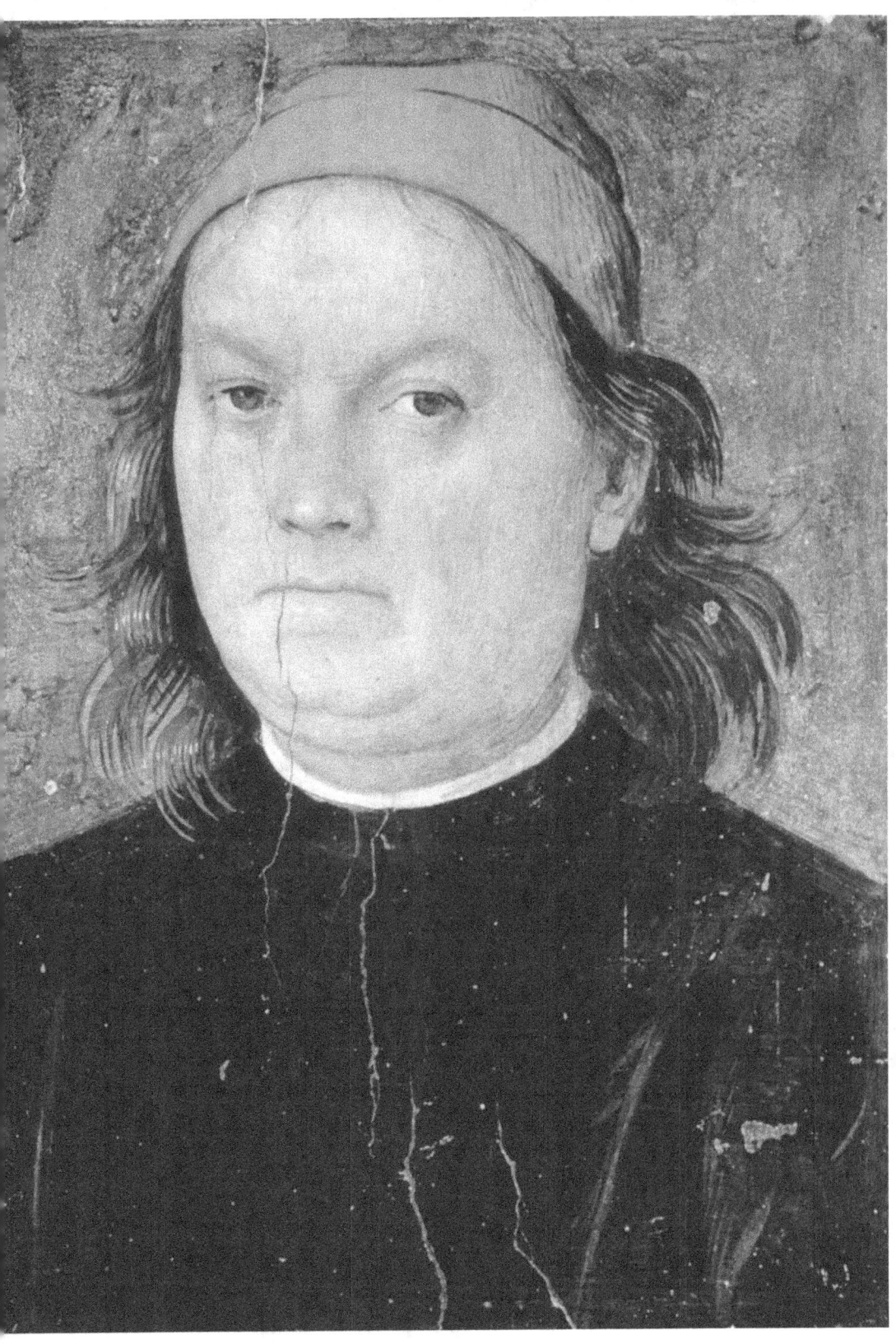

Portrait of Perugino, 1500, Perugia

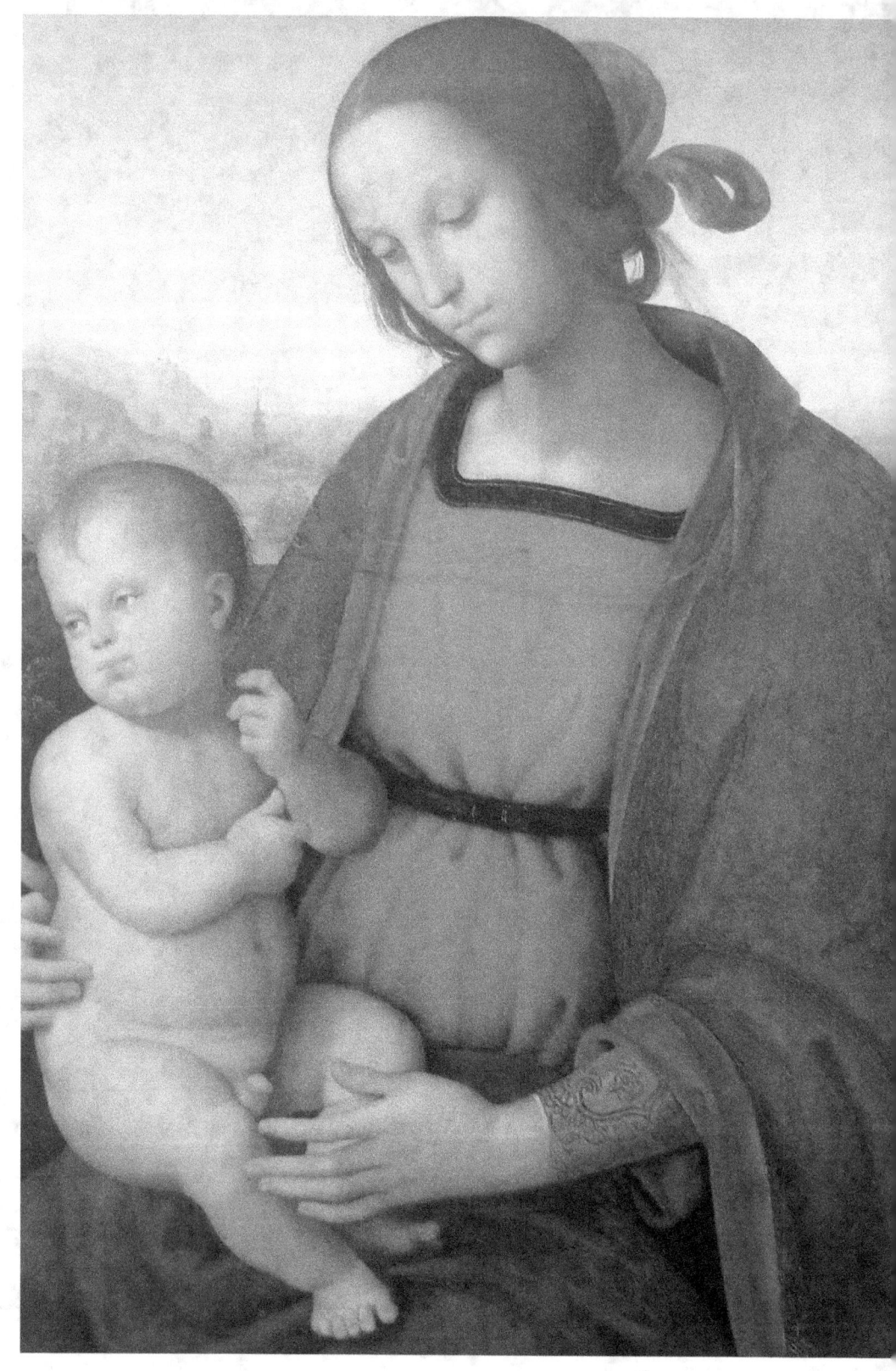

Perugino, Madonna and Child, Washington, DC

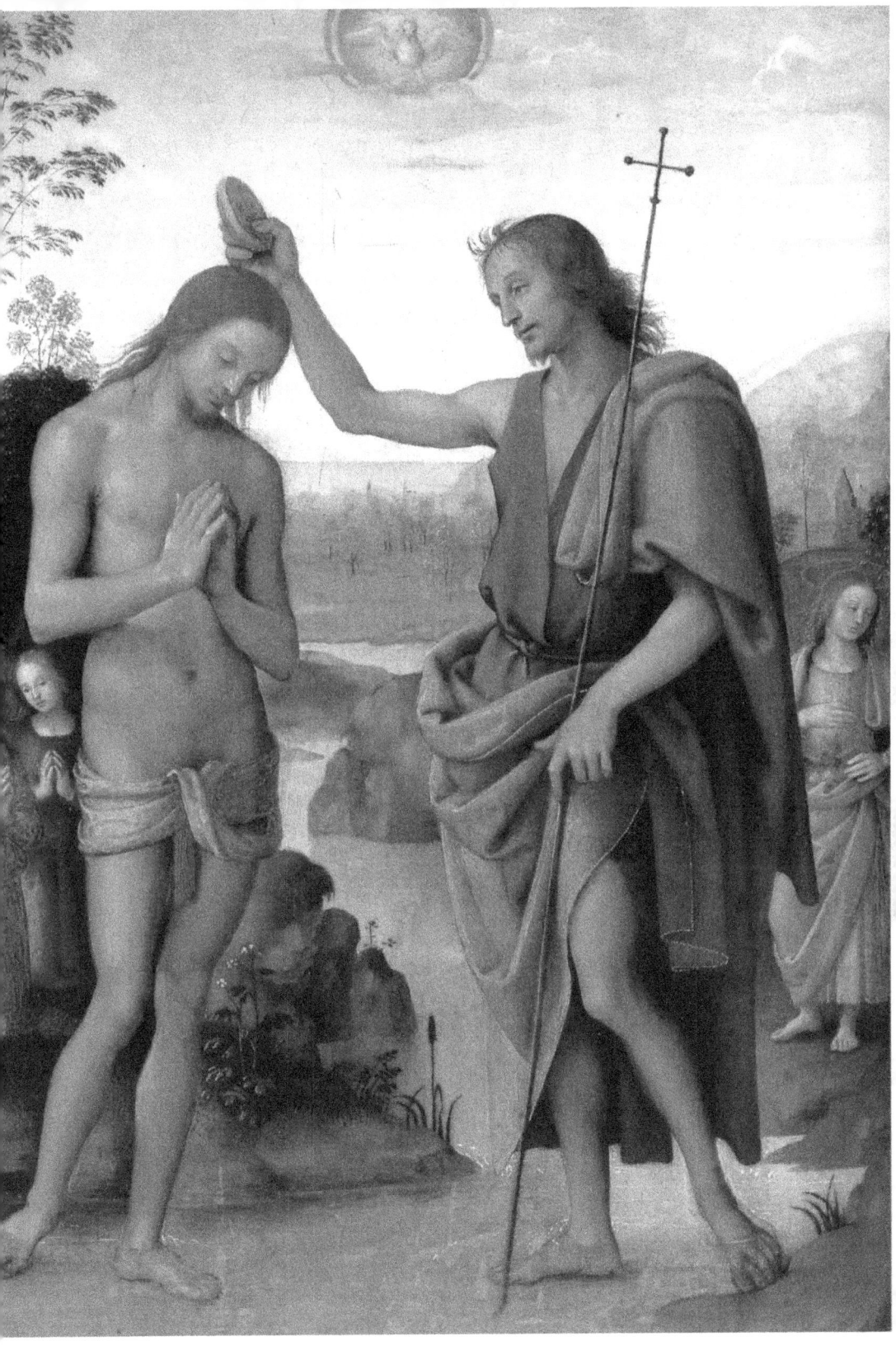

Perugino, The Baptism of Christ, 1498, Vienna

PREFACE

The following pages contain what is, I believe, the only full account of the life and works of Perugino in the English language. It is based upon a careful examination of almost every one of his works to be found in Europe, and upon a critical study of their characteristics. The labours of other investigators have, however, been laid under contribution, and I am especially indebted to the works of Crowe and Cavalcaselle, Morelli, Mariotti, Orsini, and Vasari, and also to the works and advice of Mr. Bernhard Berenson, Mrs. Herringham, and Dr. Laurie, and to the writings and researches of M. Broussolle. To the Archbishop of Trebizond (Monsignore Stonor) I am most grateful for obtaining permission for me to study the Albani altar-piece, and to Prince Torlonia for kindly granting my request, and also to His Excellency Lord Currie for constant and never-failing aid in regard to all the other Italian galleries. Signor Cecchetti has helped me to obtain good photographs of the pictures in and near to Città della Pieve, Miss Fearon has kindly re-measured some of the Italian pictures for me, and the Rev. H. R. Ware, and the Rev. T. C Robson, have given me much help in rendering the Latin verse of Perugino into English verse. To each and all of these I offer my hearty thanks. I have also to thank the Directors of the Vatican and Perugia galleries for special facilities afforded me; Mr. Murray for permission to quote from his handbooks, and the photographers for the use of their photographs, and finally to beg that if by chance I have made use of other material without the fullest acknowledgment, the omission may be forgiven me inasmuch as I have endeavoured to avoid so serious a fault. My own divergences from the accepted views will be found fully recorded in these pages, and are in every case founded upon personal study, and for them I alone am responsible.

G. C. W.

CHAPTER I

BIRTH, MASTERS,
AND ENVIRONMENT

It is not quite certain when Pietro Vannucci (called from the name of his adopted town Perugino) was born, but the place of his birth he himself announces in his signature. Probably his birth took place in 1446 or 1447 at the little town of Castello della Pieve, now called Città della Pieve, as it was raised to the dignity of a city in 1601 by Clement VIII. His signature preserves, in the words "Petrus de Castro Plebis," the older name of his birthplace. Vasari gives his father's name as Christofano, and tells us that he was a poor man; but Mariotti reminds[*A] his correspondent that the family, although a poor one, was not of low condition, as it had enjoyed the rights of citizenship since 1427. He also mentions that one Pietro Vannucci was in 1424 a member of the Guild of Stone-workers, and that in 1428 a member of the family signed himself proudly as citizen of Perugia. It is probable that Vasari's story of the boy having been brought into Perugia at a tender age and put as shop drudge with a painter in that city is correct. Città della Pieve is not more than some twenty-five miles from Perugia, and although the town is near to Chiusi, yet Perugia, as the capital of the district of Umbria, is the more important place, and to it naturally would the lad be taken. Vasari speaks of the unknown painter to whom the youthful Pietro Vannucci was sent as one who "was not particularly distinguished in his calling, but who held the art in great veneration and highly honoured the men who excelled therein."

It would be very interesting to know the name of this painter, as, according to Vasari, he had great influence upon Pietro. "He did not cease," Vasari continues, "to set before Pietro the great advantages and honours that were to be obtained from painting by all who acquired the power of labouring in it effectually, and kindled in the mind of his pupil the desire to become one of those masters." We enter upon a curious speculation when we begin to surmise the name of this master. Lanzi speaks of an artist known as Pietro of Perugia, but conjectures that Niccolò of Foligno (known also as Niccolò Liberatore, and incorrectly as Niccolò Alunno) may have been Perugino's first master. Mariotti attaches much more importance to the early teaching of Bonfigli. Fanelli, quoted by Lupattelli,[*B] speaks of "a poor and obscure youth from Città della Pieve in the school of Alunno receiving instruction from Niccolò Alunno and becoming eventually the immortal Perugino, master of Raffaello." Crowe and Cavalcaselle take Bonfigli as this early master, while later writers, notably Mr. Berenson, attach far more importance to the training of Fiorenzo di Lorenzo.

Leaving out of consideration for a space the question of what Perugino learned from Piero della Francesca and in the botegas of Florence, it maybe well to briefly glance at the influences already named.

Niccolò da Foligno was perhaps the originator of the school of Umbrian painters in which Perugino thereafter took so important a place. He was clearly a pupil of Benozzo Gozzoli, who derived his training from Beato Angelico; but into the sweetness, harmony, and tender feeling of these earlier masters Niccolò forced a fiercer spirit, an uncompromising realism, which is at times almost painful in its stress. Niccolò was a man of forceful spirit, earnest and powerful, and with a certain dry technique and rigid definition that is in full accord with the penetrating spirit that composed the pictures. Foligno is quite close to Perugia, and there is no difficulty in realising the presence of Niccolò at times in that city. His influence is marked in Perugino's early work, but it does not stand alone, and has associated with it characteristics that could not have come from the Folignate botega. Bonfigli (Benedetto Buonfiglio), to whom Vasari once refers at the conclusion of his life of Pinturicchio, was the prominent painter of Perugia. He was greatly esteemed in that city, and so largely confined his labours to his native place that even now it is impossible, save in the gallery of that city, to gain anything like an adequate knowledge of his art.

It was not, however, from Bonfigli that we consider the strong influence came that affected Perugino's work. Much of Bonfigli's work was quite beautiful; there is a fascinating grace about many of his figures; there is a tenacious hold upon the laws of perspective, rich, varied, and charming colouring, and a general pleasing result in composition and in effect. There is, however, little virile force, very slight depth of feeling, and, above all, an absence of the open space which is so characteristic of later Umbrian art, and which has such a wondrous effect in the pictures of the great Umbrian artists. Bonfigli's pictures are crowded, Perugino's never were crowded. Bonfigli's are illustrations, records, decorative effects ever full of figures, and of detail, and with the beauty of certain single faces or separate groups swamped by the crowd of ordinary objects. Perugino's pictures, whatever may be their faults, never deserve this condemnation.

Fiorenzo di Lorenzo on the contrary, must certainly have been a master from whom Perugino received no slight influence.

Once again it is needful to go to Perugia in order to study the works of this artist, as away from the hill-top city the pictures of Fiorenzo di Lorenzo, are few and far between.

In England there is one that is noteworthy, a "Virgin and Child," belonging to Mr. George Salting.

In the works of this artist we are at once struck by the aloofness that distinguished Perugino. Single figures stand apart one from the other, each slightly connected as by a thread of thought, and similarly each with the central feature of the picture, but in every other way self-contained. Here again are the placid Umbrian landscapes with which later on we shall become so familiar, and the tall slender youths and sweet women full of tender grace, that make their first appearance in Umbrian art. There is a grace and charm in the work of Fiorenzo di Lorenzo, that is far removed both from the fierce truth of the Folignate's pictures and from the crowded stress of Bonfigli, and those panels that tell the story of Bernardino in the Accademia at Perugia, and which represent the artist at his very best, are possessed of a fascination both in line, in colouring, and in movement that are impressive to the highest degree.

Occasionally the artist was able to attach two or more of his figures to one another by a gesture or a movement that formed a distinct and noticeable link; but it was left for Perugino to still further develop this power and to link his figures one by one into a single group when he so desired, or at his will to keep them aloof one from the other, and to the successors of Perugino to complete this power which Fiorenzo so slightly commenced and which Perugino so greatly improved. In another way can be seen the influence of Fiorenzo di Lorenzo. The typical Umbrian landscapes which are so important a feature in Perugino's pictures first make their appearance in the works of this artist. The special treatment of the landscape will be referred to in fuller detail later on; but we may here mention that those expansive broad landscapes, with distant hills bathed in a blue mist and revealing long stretches of level fertile land on either side, with single trees, standing silhouetted against the sky, which, like a vast arch of blue, frames in the lovely scene, are noteworthy in Fiorenzo's pictures.

Finally, there is the pale golden sunlight to be seen in his works, a sunlight which bathes all purely Umbrian art, but which does not appear to any marked extent in the works of the Foligno school.

Having now briefly glanced at the leading characteristics of these artists, it will be well to examine the work of one who was far greater than either of those already named, and whose influence on Perugino is very marked. I allude to Piero della Francesca. Whether, as Morelli suggests, Perugino journeyed to Arezzo, where Piero was at work, and aided him in his work, or placed himself under his tuition, or whether Perugino met Piero at Borgo San Sepolcro or in Perugia, is immaterial. It will suffice to understand that, somewhere near at home, and in the early days of his training before Perugino journeyed to Florence, the two men must have met, and Perugino learned much from the Tuscan-Umbrian master and profited largely by his instruction.

One of the main features of Piero's art was his accurate knowledge of perspective. He was, above all, a mathematician, well versed in arithmetic and geometry, and the author of several treatises on the science.

He rejoiced in complicated problems of perspective, in long vistas of columns stretching away into the far distance, in mysterious hollows, in exquisite alcoves, curves, and embrasures, in the perfectly accurate drawing of roofs and rooms, and in the grouping of his figures in such geometric array and such careful receding proportion as made clear the charm that such mathematical arrangements had over the mind of the artist.

There are, however, other characteristics of Piero's work, that must be carefully noted in making a survey of his style. There is a wonderful gravity and solemnity about his figures, a preoccupied look in most of their faces, and we trace also the very beginning of that power already mentioned, of linking figure to figure and group to group.

Certainly, in the long processions that form so essential a part of the frescoes at San Francesco in Arezzo, there is a certain connection running through the group of figures which are arranged in processional order especially in the "Visit of the

Queen of Sheba," the "Invention of the Cross," and the "Exaltation of the Cross," but individually the figures composing these groups are separate and distinct from one another, engaged in their own concerns and holding no converse one with the other. In these respects it was left for the later men, beginning with Perugino, to pull the picture together and make it one harmonious whole.

When to this aloofness, this curious want of sympathy between the central group or scene in the picture and all the attendant groups or figures, we add a severe absence of emotion, an impassiveness in the faces of all the figures, together with a simple dignity of style and a power of delineation that is very attractive, we begin to understand Piero della Francesca. He never considered whether the faces of his figures were specially suited to the group in which he used them. He is quite unmoved by any ideas that the spectator may have as to fitness in the picture, and he never reveals his own views as to the scene and its appropriate presentation. Rage, pity, scorn, amazement, jealousy, passion, or even the depth of devotion, are no part of Piero's repertoire, but a quiet self-contained hauteur, a learned solemnity, and a religious calm characterise his figures, both men and women. There is abundance of dignity, stately form, earnest but impassive determination, but, even in the battle scenes, nothing of the *Sturm und Drang* which would have been expected.

All these characteristics had direct influence upon Perugino, but even beyond them can be seen other marks of this master's tuition. The fantastic head-dresses that are to be seen in Piero's frescoes find their counterpart in the frescoes of the Cambio; the very same scheme of composition in "The Resurrection of Christ" in the Borgo San Sepolcro Gallery is to be seen in one of Perugino's pictures; and the long vistas of arches and careful geometric proportion and the absolutely accurate drawing of arches and columns are to be equally realised in Piero's picture in the Gallery at Perugia and in Perugino's altar-piece in the Villa

Albani. Even in the shape of the hand, the clear cameo-like profile of the faces, and the detail of the feathers on the angels' wings, the relationship between these painters is marked, and comparison between the frescoes at Arezzo and the paintings in the Accademia will be found to reveal these and other points of close contact.

In these early days of Perugino's life, it is therefore to the influence of Niccolò Liberatore, of Fiorenzo di Lorenzo, and, above all, of Piero della Francesca, that we attribute the growth of his art and the success of his later life.

One more artist he must have met in these days, as Luca Signorelli, who was some five years his senior, was probably at Arezzo with Piero della Francesca. Certain pictures of Perugino, notably the "Crucifixion," at La Calza, and the similar scene painted around a carved crucifix now at Perugia, the "Pietà" in the Accademia, and the "Love and Chastity" in Paris, betray in their vigour, hardness, and movement some of Signorelli's influence, an influence that only occasionally was to be seen in the great Umbrian master.

Morelli[*C] considers that Perugino's journey to Florence after his Perugian training, of which Vasari speaks, took place in 1470, at which time Perugino would be about twenty-five years old. His name is recorded in the roll of St. Luke in 1472, and in the roll of the Physicians in 1499.

Vasari states that it was to Verrocchio that he went. Lanzi and Orsini confirm this; Morelli gravely doubts it; Resta distinctly denies it; Berenson rejects it; and certainly there is but little trace of such a tutor in Perugino's work.

In the "Baptism" at the Accademia, which is an absolutely authentic picture, although perhaps partly the work of Leonardo, and in the "Madonna and Child" in the Uffizi, also attributed to Verrocchio, we find nothing that would appear to have influenced Perugino, or that can be recalled by his work, but if the magnificent bronze panel in the Carmine Church at Venice is accepted as the work of Andrea del Verrocchio then there is evidently a feeling in this work such as Perugino would naturally have appreciated, and which does appear many times in pictures by the Umbrian master. The position of the Christ on the ground, and that of the women who bend over Him, the silent meditative devotion of the two men and of the child who kneel on the right, the attitude, wings, drapery, and movement of the flying angels, and their very position with regard to the cross, all find answering echoes in Perugino's work that are unmistakable in their clearness. What is, however, of special importance to notice at this juncture is that Perugino did not go to Florence in 1472 as a mere pupil or scholar. Young in years as he undoubtedly was, he must have also been mature in experience and in knowledge; for otherwise it is inconceivable that so sagacious a Pontiff as Sixtus IV. should have sent for him eight years afterwards and engaged him upon work in the Sistine Chapel.

Vasari specially states that the invitation was given because of Perugino's great fame throughout Italy, and it is clear that a request to work side by side with such men as Ghirlandajo, Cosimo Rosselli, and Botticelli was so high a compliment that it would not be given to one who was merely a student in Verrocchio's botega. There is no question about the date of this invitation, as the original contract between the Holy Father and the artists has been published, and it contains an undertaking to furnish "ten stories" between October 27, 1481, and March 15, 1482.

Prior to these dates we hear of two other works executed by Perugino. The earliest of all is recorded by Milanesi in his notes to the life in Vasari. He states that in 1475 Perugino was commissioned to paint certain frescoes in the Palazzo Publico in Perugia; but of these works not a trace remains, and there is no evidence to support the learned author's statement [*D] Milanesi, moreover, further records the fact that in 1478 Perugino worked at Cerqueto, painting some frescoes in a chapel there, and one solitary figure of "San Sebastian" bearing that date only now remains out of the entire decoration.

To this interesting figure (*St Sebastian* 1478), the earliest known work of the master, a reference will be made later on when consideration is given to other representations of the same saint, but a record must here be made to the Foligno, and to the Signorelli influence that this figure betrays. In direct truth the figure might well be the work of Niccolò Liberatore, and is conceived on the lines of his school. In nervous, tense muscular representation, and in the movement of the limbs, it is strikingly Signorellesque, and the realism of its wounds bespeaks the same characteristic; but the silky treatment of the skin, the roundness of the limbs, the upturned piteous face, the locks of hair, the extraordinarily exaggerated size of the great toe, and, above all, the intricate puckered folds of the drapery, are Perugino's and Perugino's alone.

The painting of the drapery which becomes a mannerism, and one of the most accurate of tests here in the very early days of the artist, takes certain definite forms, and the dark hollows and curious hook-like folds are to be seen in this "San Sebastian," not certainly as freely but quite as definitely, as they appear in later days. The picture is but a fragment of what must have been an important fresco, but it is eloquent of better work to come, and shows promise of masterly execution that only three years afterwards was to be revealed at Rome in the Sistine Chapel. No other work exists to bridge over the time between Perugino's early training in Umbria, his sojourn in Florence, and his return as a well-known artist to the town and neighbourhood of Perugia, although there is said to be a picture near Naples dated 1460, but the date is probably apocryphal.

In Florence the artist would probably have met Leonardo da Vinci and Lorenzo di Credi. If he attended at Verrocchio's studio he certainly would have met them. In Florence also, Resta tells us, he studied Masaccio's work, and we may be quite sure he used every endeavour to perfect himself in his art; and it is to this period of residence that Giovanni Santi refers in his oft quoted lines:

"Due giovin par d'etate e par d'amori
Leonardo da Vinci e P Perusino
Pier della Pieve."

– "Two youths alike in age and love Leonardo di Vinci and
the Perugian Peter of Pieve." He is mentioned in Florence in 1490
in one of the books relating to the Cathedral, and there is a story
of his having been fined for fighting in Florence in 1488.

In the only picture that remains to us of the series executed by
Perugino in Rome for Sixtus IV. we see the result of all this
Florence training, but we are also confronted at once by the great
characteristic of the Umbrian school – free open space.

In considering this great feature, the most noteworthy
characteristic of Umbrian art, it is impossible to avoid reference to
Mr. Bernhard Berenson's pages and to his definition of what he
terms "space composition," which he defines in this way:

"Space composition differs from ordinary composition in the first
place most obviously in that it is not an arrangement to be judged as
extending only laterally, or up and down, on a flat surface, but as
extending inwards in depth as well. It is composition in three
dimensions and not in two, in the cube and not merely on the
surface." [*E]

Farther on he remarks:

"This art comes into existence only when we get a sense of space not
as a void, as something merely negative such as we customarily have,
but on the contrary as something very positive and definite, able to
confirm our consciousness of being, to heighten our feeling of
vitality."

It is the wonderful art of space compositions which so
distinguishes Perugino from his Sistine Chapel days down to the
end of his life.

The power is so well expressed by Mr. Berenson that nothing
is needed to further define it but he still further emphasises
"space composition" when he states that it is an "intrinsically

religious art" capable of "communicating the religious emotion" and able to "awaken in those who looked at the pictures a consciousness of preference for a life holy and refined."

In this first great picture "Christ giving the Keys to St. Peter," all the power of this marvellous capability is at once apparent.

It produces a sense of vastness, of spaciousness, of broad, free, open air enclosed only by the blue arch of Heaven, and therefore gathers up and retains all the higher emotions of the spectator.

There are the grand figures in the foreground, majestic and wonderful in their dignity; beyond them are others in the receding distance, smaller and smaller as the eye notes the vast distance expressed in the picture. In the centre rises the wonderful temple. Bramantesque and stately, and beyond it, disappearing away into the horizon are the everlasting hills that bound and yet seem to extend the broad space of the Umbrian landscape the utmost distance of which is lost in the blue haze of the sky.

The two triumphal arches at the sides serve to emphasise the great space that the picture embraces and the effect is that of gazing through an open window in Perugia or at Montefalco.

There is no sense of crowding, the space is so vast that the populace of a country could not crowd it, and the air circulates in and around every group and serves to give the greater *plein-air* charm.

There is a soothing quiet about the whole, a self-restraint and a stillness, and even though figure stands apart from figure and each one hardly notices the other, yet there is a fine thread of common interest to be seen connecting the whole of the foreground group and linking the spectators to the two central persons, Christ and the Foundation of His Church.

It is well when mentioning this great picture to state as a personal opinion that it is not possible to appreciate Perugino adequately, or even to understand him properly, without a visit to Umbria itself.

The country differs so much from other parts of Italy that mere comparison with parts better known is useless, but when once the student has sojourned in the country the charm of its landscape is felt and understood. There is a vastness about its open spaces, an immensity of view, boundless and yet enclosed, that must be seen to be understood.

To linger on the fortifications of Montefalco, to look out from the public square of Trevi, to wander along the road that divides San Girolamo from Spello, to drive along the plains of Foligno, to stay at Nervi, Deruta, or Bettona, to gaze out over the plains around Assisi, or to appreciate the wonderland that is mapped out around lofty Perugia – all these are so many lessons to the right understanding of Perugino. Away and away in the rolling distance are those vast plains, not flat surfaces, but a luxuriant country-side, irregularly marked by the contours of hills and valleys, dotted with tiny fortified towns crowning each its own hill and looking down upon its neighbour. Great white winding roads meander hither and thither, single trees stand out in sharp tall silhouette against the intense blue of the sky, and around as far as eye can reach stretch the half-hidden, half-revealed mountains clothed in a purple haze while the golden glare of sunlight bathes all the intervening space in its mystic light, tinging with gold the very grass of the fields, the grey drab of the roads, the ruddy brown of the buildings, and the radiance of the distant towers and houses.

All the Umbrian artists felt the charm of this scenery, but no one save Perugino so fully and so consistently expressed it.

It is in all his works, and as one gazes out upon this "buoyant spaciousness" of view, the wondrous creatures of his conceptions, holy women, saints, prophets, apostles, religious guilds, praying populace, seem once more to people the earth, and away in the eternal immeasurable sky can be seen the Assumption, the angels, the mandorla of cherub faces, the comforting seraphim and the glowing cherubim, as Perugino saw them, and the sky is again the scene of the glories which faith enabled Perugino to visualise and depict.

It is the knowledge of his own country and the wonderful

power of space composition that marks Perugino's pictures so emphatically as to enable us to determine that the "Delivery of the Keys to St. Peter" is the only fresco from the master's hand in the Sistine Chapel. It was Morelli who first pointed out that Crowe and Cavalcaselle were in error in attributing "Moses and Zipporah" and the "Baptism of Christ" to Perugino, and I accept his teaching in this matter quite readily. A careful study of the Sistine frescoes has convinced me that Morelli was right and Crowe and Cavalcaselle wrong. Even the two central figures in the disputed "Baptism," those of Christ and St. John, which are compared with the two similar figures in the predella at Rouen, which is undoubtedly authentic, and with the same scene in the National Gallery, which I consider a copy only of the master's work, betray the hand of Pinturicchio rather than that of Perugino.

In the fresco at Rome, the two figures are crowded closely together; the arm of Our Lord almost rests on St. John's head, the face of the saint is weak and feeble, the limbs are skinny and badly drawn, there is no sense of security in the feet, the hands are out of proportion and the draperies entirely lack the hook folds of Perugino, and are loose and inadequate. Above all, neither figure stands upon its two feet; in the case of the Christ one foot alone supports the whole body, a mistake that Perugino never makes. The whole picture is crowded with figures and hemmed in with hills. It is pictorial certainly, and effective, but it entirely lacks the spaciousness of Perugino. There is a feeling of crush and crowd such as Perugino never gives, and a total absence even in the landscape of that extensive vista of scenery, that breadth of treatment which is so important. Even the representation of the Eternal Father within the mandorla of cherubs and attended by angels is not placed high up in the illimitable aerial space, but almost touches a neighbouring hill, and serves but to overfill the picture and make its crowded composition a wearisome burden. Compare for a moment the predella at Rouen. The two central figures stand apart one from the other, and therefore stand out clearly and distinctly, while yet near enough for their mutual actions to be closely connected. They stand firmly and well balanced on their feet, the slight exaggeration of one of St. John's feet, being due to an accurate understanding on Perugino's part of the distortion apparently given to the limb by its being below the surface of the water. Around are the kneeling angels and attendant figures, eight only in number, carefully graduated in size according to position, aloof, serious, quiet, and still. Away and beyond is the rolling landscape, with its exquisite hills and dainty detached trees standing out clear against the sky. On and on the eye travels, eager to reach the limits of this limitless vision, and impressed more and more by the skill that painted in so tiny a compass so vast a scene. Above is the sky free from any crowd of spirits, and reaching up to unimagined heights.

Here is undoubtedly Perugino's work; but at Rome we see merely a clever overcrowded picture, an illustration simply, and most evidently the work of Pinturicchio. Three other frescoes in this chapel Perugino did undoubtedly paint for Sixtus IV., covering the eastern wall. They depicted the "Assumption," into which he introduced the kneeling figure of the Pope, the "Nativity," and the "Finding of Moses," but all these works were swept away during the Pontificate of Pope Paul III. to make way for the tremendous work of Michel Angelo, "The Last Judgment." It is infinitely to be regretted that no replica of these frescoes was retained, as the "Delivery of the Keys" is so superb a composition, that it but increases the desire of the spectator to know what Perugino's other frescoes were in the same chapel.

The payment for the frescoes in the Sistine Chapel was not authorised till August 8th, 1489, as Mariotti [*F] records that at that time Perugino was entitled to draw on the Apostolic *camera* at Perugia for 180 ducats, being the balance of money due for pictures in the Apostolic chapel. On the 5th of March 1490 Perugino gave a receipt in Perugia for that money.

CHAPTER II

EARLY DAYS

There are three pictures, one of which is especially named by Crowe and Cavalcaselle, which seem to belong to the early days of Perugino.

Not that they should be ascribed to the Cerqueto period, or to the Sistine Chapel time, but it is probable that they were painted between 1480, when the master was in Rome, and 1491, when he produced on his second journey to the Eternal City the magnificent altar-piece now in the Villa Albani. Crowe and Cavalcaselle refer to the tondo in the Louvre, and to it we add the somewhat similar work at Verona and the "Baptism" at Vienna.

There is a certain immaturity in these three pictures, a straining after effect, a poorness in colouring, and a rigidity in the draperies, together with a niggling technique, with hard tight outlines, that was to give place so speedily to far more breadth. At the same time, thus early, if my surmise as to date is correct, can be seen the characteristics of Perugino. All three pictures are full of *plein-air* effect, the one at Verona especially. The group in Paris of "Madonna and Child" with two saints and two angels is a little cramped and crowded. The Verona one omits the two saints and introduces as another child St. John Baptist.

In the Vienna "Baptism," which has been repainted in places, there is a hardness in the draperies, a stiffness in the attendant figures, and an unfinished character to the landscape; but in each of the three there is sweetness, calm, and devotion, and they mark the beginning of quite a new movement in Italian art. It will be noticed that both in Paris and Verona the under draperies are regular and hard in their pleating, that the head-dresses are merely conventional and stiffly angular and that ornaments, decoration, and jewellery have received an amount of fine laborious detail work, which renders them somewhat too conspicuous, and shows that the artist had not yet realised the sense of proportion in the various parts of his pictures that distinguished him later on.

From consideration of these three pictures, remarkably interesting and thoroughly typical as they are of the new school of work just unfolding, it will be well to pass on to more definite ground and consider some dated pictures which follow in due course.

There is an amusing story in Mariotti respecting one masterpiece that should be mentioned here. The Priori of Perugia desired to have an important altar-piece for their Capella dell' Magistrato, and in the predella of the picture, or else introduced into the altar-piece itself, were to be the portraits of the worthy Priori.

A local artist, one Pietro di Maestro Galeotto, was selected for the work, and on the 7th of June 1479 a contract was made with him for it, the price to be 200 florins, and the picture to be completed in two years under a fine for non-compliance of 50 golden ducats. Galeotto from time to time drew payments on account from the Priori, and three years passed away and yet there were no signs of the altar-piece and no mention of the fine. On June 29th, 1482, another year's grace was granted to Galeotto on the plea that there had been some contagious disease in Perugia and he had struck work and absented himself; but in May 1483 Galeotto died, whether from this plague or not is not recorded, but when inquiry was made of his heirs as to the picture nothing could be found of it but the frame. Shortly after this time Perugino visited Perugia, and to him the Magistrates turned for help; and, bringing much pressure to bear upon him, prevailed upon the artist to sign a contract dated 28th November 1483 binding himself to produce the picture in four months for 100 florins. The details of the picture are all given in the contract, and the names of the four Saints, who were to surround the Madonna and Child, and, above all, the portraits of the Priori were not to be omitted. But by this time Perugino had received the commands of Pope Sixtus IV. to come to Rome, and so a few days after signing the contract Perugino left Perugia without giving any further consideration to the wishes of the worthy Priori or the text of the contract. Even the first section of the work, containing the portraits which he had faithfully promised should be ready in December 1483, was quite forgotten.

The term of office, however, for which the Priori were elected was rapidly nearing its close, and there were still no signs of the portraits of these eminent men. In despair the Priori turned to a third artist, Santi di Polonio del Celandro, and in a contract dated 31st December 1483 they bound him to supply the picture and complete it within a year, but inserted a clause that all the portraits together with that of their notary were to be painted within a fortnight.

For the whole work he was to have one hundred florins. This time the Priori kept their eye on the artist; there was no time to lose. Shortly they would go out of office, and then the chance of having their portraits forever adorning their chapel walls would be gone, and so the poor Celandro had to paint the eleven portraits within fifteen days, under pain of a very heavy fine. Somehow or other he accomplished the work; the portraits were done, and temporarily remained in the chapel standing against the wall waiting for the completion of the rest of the pictures. But, having accomplished this part of the work, Celandro took no further heed of the contract, and the Priori having obtained their desire, troubled no further as to the Madonna and saints, or were powerless to force Celandro to complete the work. Twelve years actually passed away, and the chapel still lacked its altar-piece, and Celandro, like Galeotto, died.[*G] In 1495 Perugino was again at Perugia, full of honour and fame; and once more the decoration of the Capella was resolved on. The Priori – quite a new body to the one which had originally planned the picture, entered into another contract with Perugino, dated 6th March 1495 – for him to paint the altar-piece on the same scheme as before, but with far higher remuneration. Perugino was to do the work in six months, was to receive one hundred gold ducats in three payments, and, in lieu of the Mother of Mercy in the lunette, was to paint a Pietà, and for that purpose – alas for the poor Priori – the portraits in fresco by Celandro which filled the space allotted to the Pietà were to be removed, broken up, and carted away. All, therefore, that remains concerning these notable Priori of 1483 whose portraits were to have been handed down to perpetuity, are their ten names recorded by Mariotti, and the name of Rubino di Giacomo, their notary; but of their portraits nothing is left.

Perugino at last set to work, and the beautiful altar-piece now in the Vatican is the result. There is the Madonna and Child on the throne, and near by there are the four great saints. The picture is exquisitely beautiful, full of Perugino's special charm, and bearing marks of the Piero della Francesca influence in the arches that support the canopy, while below the feet of the Madonna, to make quite clear as to who painted the picture, is the signature in somewhat remarkable form:

HOC PETRUS DE CHASTRO PLEBIS PINXIT.

Inasmuch as consideration of this finished picture brings our chronological survey up to 1495, it will be desirable for us to retrace our steps to the time that Perugino spent in Florence.

Vasari records many works executed in that city, but his chronology is so perplexing that it is difficult to say whether they were all executed at the time to which we refer, or later in the artist's career.

Probably the frescoes in the Convent of the Frati-Gesuati beyond the Pinti Gale, a house that was destroyed in the siege of Florence in 1529, were early works, inasmuch as the panel pictures that were saved from the church, and which now rest in the Accademia, were painted in 1492-93.

There were, however, as already mentioned, three pictures on panel executed for the same convent, and these, fortunately, are still in existence. They were carried, at the time of the siege, to the gate of San Pier Gattolini, where the monks were provided with a refuge in the church and convent of San Giovannino, now known as La Calza. These three pictures are the "Crucifixion," now in La Calza, the "Pietà," in the Accademia, dated 1493, and the "Christ in the Garden," also in the Accademia. Of these three early pictures the one in La Calza is in some ways the most interesting. It is a very puzzling picture. Vasari describes it so clearly that there is no possibility of error as to the picture he names. He speaks of the "infinite care" with which it is executed. He refers to its being carried for safety to the church, where it still rests, and he mentions its condition as injured by numerous cracks, but the difficulty is that, while much of the picture is distinctly Peruginesque, three of the figures might have been painted by Luca Signorelli, so great a resemblance in general characteristics do they bear to his work. Crowe and Cavalcaselle hesitate to ascribe it to either master, inclining more to the view that Raffaelino del Garbo may have painted it, but with this last ascription I cannot at all agree. The composition is that of Perugino, the open air effect and the distance, the single detached trees and the high rocks are all Umbrian. The draperies of the four standing figures and of the Christ have the distinctive folds that are so thoroughly characteristic of our painter, and the borders to the garments are equally noteworthy. The attitude of St. Francis and of S. Giovanni Columbini are thoroughly in accordance with Perugino's methods, but when we turn to St. Jerome and St. John Baptist the case is very different. In these figures the fierce strength and muscular development is foreign to Perugino's ordinary work, and he appears to have been painting under Signorelli's influence, and even endeavouring to introduce into faces and limbs the virile power and movement of Signorelli, which at that time was specially attractive to him. The figure of the Magdalen (strangely termed by Crowe and Cavalcaselle the best figure in the picture) is, I consider, a much later addition by quite another hand. The picture composes perfectly without it, and a very close inspection convinced me that it was not originally in the design, and that the draperies of S. Giovanni Columbini can be traced through the draperies of the Magdalen. In no way does the Magdalen recall Perugino. The attitude is not his; the draperies have entirely different folds; the hands are quite different in their structure; and the hair is painted with entirely altered technique.

I look upon this La Calza "Crucifixion" as one of the earliest, if not the very first of Perugino's works in Florence that survives.

In the Accademia (two pictures) we are on quite different ground. Here can be seen the hand of Perugino in every part and the wonderful power of space composition can be realised to the full. The receding arches in the "Pietà," bespeaking the influence of Piero della Francesca, the exquisite landscape in the background, the curious aloofness of each figure, and the delicate chain of sympathy that binds them all together, the tender sorrowful face of the Madonna seated in the midst bearing on her knees the dead body of her Son, all of Perugino's best.

The third picture, the "Christ in the Garden," is fuller still of the genius of space composition. Far off are the hills that girdle the landscape, and the eye is carried on from one to the other, each step revealing new beauties, till in the extreme distance the sky and land melt into one another. In the immediate foreground are the three disciples sound asleep in the attitudes that convince you of heavy slumber. In the centre of the picture is Our Lord kneeling on a hillock deeply engaged in prayer, and above is an angel flying toward Him bearing the chalice of sorrow. Below and still further removed from the eye of the spectator are groups of soldiers on the one hand and of priests and people on the other rapidly moving toward the central figure. Their proportions are finely adjusted to their distance and position, and there is an admirable sense of movement in all. Beyond them are the distant town, the hills, the country, and above, with its depth and arch and vastness, suggested in most subtle manner by the light fleecy clouds and by the very curves of the angel's figure and the movement of his wing rises the blue vault of the heaven.

All the genius of Perugino exists in this picture. Later on there is a greater sweetness in some of the faces, there are more figures, there is a purer and more exquisitely sunny colouring, but in composition this early work contains all the characteristics of the master.

These two must be attributed, however, to a later period than the frescoes and La Calza picture already mentioned, which were for the same convent, and in the interval between painting the frescoes for the Gesuati and the La Calza picture and these two Accademia pictures, Perugino had declined a commission at Orvieto, and had been to Rome and painted there for Cardinal Giuliano della Rovere, afterwards Julius II.

Once more we must retrace our steps and tell the story of the Orvieto contract.

It is unnecessary to refer to the work done in Orvieto Cathedral by Beato Fra Angelico; but after his death the work remained unfinished, and the authorities of the cathedral could not find anyone who was prepared to complete the scheme of decoration and whose work appeared to them worthy of its place. Forty-four years had passed away, and then Perugino visited Orvieto. He was asked to examine the chapel and give a price for its decoration. He did so; at 1500 gold ducats for the whole chapel, provided that scaffolding, lime, gold, and ultramarine were furnished to him. He agreed to use such subjects as were submitted to him, and to personally execute the hands and faces of all the figures. His offer was not accepted in its entirety; but a contract was made for him to do the ceilings and spaces above the capitals for 200 gold ducats, ten of which were paid him, on the understanding that he began the work in April 1490 and continued it through the whole of the following summer. Perugino, however, having secured the contract, was in no hurry to fulfil it, and as the question was being discussed in Florence as to the completion of the cathedral west front, he left Orvieto, and hurried on to Florence to compete in the proposed work.

The work in Florence, however, did not come off, and Perugino proceeded to Perugia and went on again to Rome. Here he commenced the work for his patron Cardinal Giuliano della Rovere, almost all of which has since perished, one notable picture only being left.

The artist seems to have dreaded lest the canons of Orvieto should demand his presence in their cathedral, and it is clear that they made strenuous efforts to lay hold of him.

The Cardinal, very desirous of retaining his services for himself, protected the artist, and when the Orvieto authorities determined to cancel the contract, he wrote to the Priori an exceedingly strong letter, telling them to await the convenience of the artist and himself. This letter of June 2, 1492, was in reply to one sent to Perugino stating that the Priori would appoint some one else in his stead.

The Cardinal reminded the authorities that they had promised, in reply to a previous letter from Perugino, to wait a few months, and he adds:

"Now Maestro Pietro has stated that, contrary to your word, you intend to substitute for him another painter who shall do your work. This is indeed truly remarkable conduct. We laboured under the impression that you were to be compliant as best suits the love we have ever borne to your community. So we now again exhort and pray that you do reserve this place, which is his due, to Maestro Pietro, and refrain from molesting him for the short time during which he has to expedite our affairs."

The Orvietans had, however, meantime, been in correspondence with Pinturicchio, but fearing to offend so great a dignitary as the Cardinal, they retained the chapel of S. Brizio for Perugino, giving Pinturicchio work in another part of the cathedral.

Perugino, however, never kept his promise, though it does not appear whether he returned to the Priori of Orvieto, the ten ducats they had advanced him, and eventually, as is well known, Luca Signorelli was employed to decorate the chapel in question.

As already mentioned, but one picture remains of the work done for the Cardinal at Rome. This is the wonderful altar-piece, dated 1491, now the property of Prince Torlonia, and to be seen in the Villa Albani.

It is in six compartments, and is a most beautiful work, full of brilliant colour. In the centre is "The Nativity," represented as having taken place beneath a sort of temple with open sides, its roof resting on a series of beautiful arches forming a centre and two aisles and springing from square pillars with rich capitals.

The three divisions above contain the "Annunciation" and "Crucifixion." On either side of the cross are St. John the Divine and the Virgin, and at its foot kneels the Magdalen. If with this figure of Mary Magdalen is compared the similar one in the La Calza picture the difference will be apparent. There is a beauty and nobility of face and a grace of posture wholly lacking in the La Calza picture, and the draperies, so sure a mark of Perugino's hand, are here as true to his method as in the Florence picture they are manifestly different. On one side of the lunette is a panel representing the Virgin kneeling beneath the open arcading of a temple, and on the opposite side a similar panel containing the Archangel Gabriel.

The altar-piece is full of the influence of Piero della Francesca, the fine drawing of the receding arches, the architectural details, the marble of the pavement and the proportion of all the figures mark in unmistakable form the teaching of the man of Arezzo, but beyond all this there is that marvellous charm of open air and composition in depth that is so marked in the best works of our

Umbrian master. The lunette gives Perugino at his best in this period, and the distance, with its rocks, pools of water, cities, plains, and hills, is of fascinating beauty, and fills the spectator with amazement. The whole picture is bathed in a haze of golden colouring. The tones, in places almost jewel-like in their transparent brilliancy, are tender and expressive, and there is a serenity and quiet about the work that is quite wonderful and expressive of complete peace and masterful resignation. The picture is signed:

PETRVS DE PERVSIA PINXIT 1491.

Now for a while we return to Florence, picking up the threads that we dropped a few pages back.

In 1493 Perugino was balloted, so Orsini says, into the municipal council at his native place, Città della Pieve, for May and June, and is said to have served his time there, but in the same year he was painting at Florence, and, according to Mariotti, had a botega in that city and accepted many commissions. To this period belong two notable pictures, one in Florence and the other in Vienna. The face of the Virgin in each picture is identical, and the infant Christ in each is painted from the same model. The picture in the Uffizi was painted for San Domenico in Fiesole, and was the second altar-piece Perugino did for that church, the first, painted in 1488, having disappeared.

It represents the Virgin on a throne bearing the infant Christ on her knees. On one side stands St. Sebastian (to whom reference will be made later on) and on the other, St. John the Baptist. The group stands under the vaulted arching resting on square pillars, of which Perugino was so fond. In the distance is the customary landscape. The picture is signed:

PETRVS PERVSINVS PINXIT AN 1493.

The other work is at Vienna, and bears an inscription

denoting the name of the priest who commissioned its execution.

The Blessed Virgin is on a throne in this picture also, but the group is enclosed by high stone walls only open to the sky. On one side stand St. John the Baptist and St. Paul, on the other, St. Jerome and St. Peter. The St. Jerome is the same face as appears in the Albani altar-piece of 1491, and the curious long white beard which he wears, and which hangs in two divisions, will be noticed many times in later works notably at Trevi and Montefalco, and constitutes a mark of Perugino's own handiwork.

CHAPTER III

TECHNIQUE: PIGMENTS: VEHICLES

We now come to the year 1494; but before dealing *seriatim* with the pictures painted at that time it will be well to refer briefly to a question of technique. Crowe and Cavalcaselle make a definite statement to which I can give no adherence. They speak of Pietro's work changing from tempera to oil work, and they allude to his inability at this time to use the new medium in all its complexity, and later on to his complete mastery over oil-painting and his constant use of it. Mr. Herbert Horne, on the other hand, states with an equal assurance that "all Perugino's pictures were painted in tempera on a gesso background,"[*H] and I find it as difficult to accept this statement as that of Crowe and Cavalcaselle as a sufficient explanation of the question.

It is quite clear to a careful observer that the technique of the Albani picture differs from that of the triptych in the National Gallery, for example; but the difficulty is then only stated. It is an extremely puzzling question to determine from an old master painting whether it was painted in tempera or not. Even Ruskin once admitted that he had for a long time been holding up for admiration as the finest oil-painting what he finally discovered to be tempera. The repeated oiling and varnishing to which Italian pictures have been submitted renders the task of discriminating the original medium one of the greatest perplexity. When to this is added the further statement that in some pictures it would appear that the under-painting which gives the shadows is in tempera and the glazes in oil colour, the danger of making such dogmatic statements as those already mentioned, is still more apparent.

The information which we possess as to tempera painting in the fourteenth century is derived from the "Trattato" of Cennino Cennini, and this has just been re-translated by the one person in England, who, more than anyone else has practised and understands tempera work. Mrs. Herringham, who has for years worked in tempera and copied the Quatrocento pictures in the National Gallery, has discussed this abstruse question, and to her knowledge, derived both from personal conversation and from her invaluable book,[*I] I have obtained much information, and have coupled it with close personal examination of the pictures, and some interesting experiments. I think, in considering tempera painting, one factor, that of climate, has not always received sufficient attention. Mr. Spencer Stanhope has expressed to Mrs. Herringham that tempera never dries completely in this country, and should not be varnished, but that has not been her experience. It, however, expresses in crude statement, the difficulty there is in this moist climate in using tempera satisfactorily, and there is little doubt that part of the success of Italian tempera work is due to the climate in which the artists worked. It is quite clear from Mrs. Herringham's work, that tempera painting, by which I mean strictly yolk-of-egg painting, is capable of the soft transparent effects which are to be seen in Perugino's pictures, and that no admixture of another vehicle with the egg is needful. It is not, however, clear whether the *whole* of many of his pictures were painted with yolk of egg alone.

I was in hopes at one time that a careful study of cracking and a comparison of the shape and formation of the cracks on different pictures would give me some definite formulæ by which the medium used could be detected, but a very careful examination only gave inadequate results. There appear to be certain thick ridge-like formations in the darker colours especially at the very edges of the draperies, which it is very difficult to imitate in tempera, and while the landscape is most clearly put in quite lightly in tempera, yet the draperies are so different in handling as to give the impression that another medium was used for them. There is also a curious variety in Perugino's pictures as to hatching, especially after 1500, and the hatching which till then only appears in the flesh, is later on to be seen in other parts of the picture. Blending of one colour with another is also to be seen in some of the later pictures to an extent that the earlier pictures never show, as with pure tempera painting the paint "cannot be moved and blended as in oil work," but "it must be put on and left alone till it is dry." I do not pretend to have touched more than the fringe of this subject, but my opinion is that Perugino did many of his pictures wholly in tempera, and that with others he used tempera for the under-painting and oil for the glazes, and that there are also pictures where size has been used as a medium for the draperies when great solidity and heavy cordy outline was desired. The question of oil colours cannot be dismissed in a sentence. Perugino probably learned a good deal as to the use of colours from the Gesuati, who were, as Vasari informs us, well practised in the art of colours, and conversant with glass-painting and enamel work, but the mystery remains as to how it is that the very fugitive colours he used have stood and remained as brilliant as ever.

For his Cantor Lectures in 1892, [*J] Dr. A.P. Laurie carried out some remarkable experiments with certain fugitive colours and certain oils and balsams, with a view to ascertaining whether any oil varnishes were impervious to moisture, and securely locked up the colours against change. Some of these experiments I have repeated, and I have had some interesting conversation with Dr. Laurie, and I agree with him absolutely that the only vehicles which lock up the colours against moisture and against the action of sulphuretted hydrogen are those composed of balsams. The stickiness of colour ground in balsam to which he alludes can, I have ascertained, be overcome by a few drops of pure linseed oil and a morsel of wax, and the result can then be used easily with a brush. Experimenting with the balsams of the larch and of the silver fir, I have been able to protect verdigris, orpiment, and kermes lake securely, and the experiments have been mainly conducted with verdigris and orpiment as notoriously fugitive colours and yet colours which it is quite clear Perugino used.

It may be well perhaps to allude here to Vasari's story respecting the artist's use of ultramarine. The colour was so costly that in several of his contracts Perugino expressly stated that his patron was to provide it, and Vasari states that when he was painting in the cloister of the Ingesuati, the Prior, who himself prepared and supplied the ultramarine, was mean and mistrustful as to Perugino's use of it, and would always be present when it was used. The artist took the Prior's distrust to heart, and by constantly washing his brush in a bowl of water allowed more colour to be precipitated than he was using in his fresco. Having punished the Prior in this way, he gathered up the blue from the water and returned it to him with the words, "This belongs to you, father; Learn to trust honest men, for such never deceive those who confide in them, although they well know how to circumvent distrustful persons like yourself when they desire to do so." Pliny records a singular story about vermilion. Perugino's skies were painted with this colour, and put on very thinly, and they have a peculiar formation of cracking which is quite recognisable.

As regards grounds, I believe that all Perugino's panel pictures are upon gesso laid upon panel, but in many of them it seems to me that linen has been used between the panel and the gesso as if to bind them together. Verdigris is, I believe, the only colour that will produce some of Perugino's greens, and, as far as I have experimented, the balsams, as Venice turpentine and olio d' abezzo, are the only varnishes that protect it unchanged against the action of sulphuretted hydrogen and moisture.

These few statements as to technique are only suggestive. I am not a chemist, and the subject demands prolonged experiments in a laboratory; and such experiments should result in most interesting discoveries. Resta calls Perugino's colouring dry and sparing; Lanzi alludes to what he terms its skimpiness, but the very thinness of it is but proof of the artist's complete mastery of his medium, and that this medium was always mainly tempera, and was never what we know as oil painting is my distinct opinion, based upon an examination of almost every one of his works in Italy.

CHAPTER IV

WANDERINGS

Crowe and Cavalcaselle, in speaking of the beautiful picture at Cremona dated 1494, refer to it as executed in Florence and sent to Cremona, but there are grave reasons against accepting this statement. It is quite clear that in that year Perugino was in Venice, [*K] and it is more natural to believe that he painted the picture in Cremona itself. The picture is one of great beauty, but is singularly unlike most of the painter's other creations in a sturdy robustness of pose and countenance, both in the Madonna and in the Child, unlike the calm and slightly insipid composure of other works. This characteristic may perhaps be attributed to the recent influence of the works of Giovanni Bellini and Antonello da Messina.

The picture represents the Blessed Virgin and Child on a throne, while St. James is on one side, St. Augustine on the other of the central figures. It is signed 1494, and still hangs in St. Augustine's Church, Cremona, on the altar of the Roncadelli family.

In 1496 the Duke Il Moro of Milan was anxious to obtain the services of another painter for the rooms at the Castello, and he wrote to his envoy in Florence for information. The envoy replied, giving to the Duke information as to the leading characteristics of each of the greater Florentine artists. Of Perugino he wrote: "He is a rare and singular artist, most excellent in wall painting. His faces have an air of the most angelic sweetness." The Duke Lorenzo at once decided to employ Perugino, and wrote to his friend Guido Arcimboldo, Archbishop of Milan, who was then in Venice, begging him to inquire about Perugino, and, if possible, engage him. The Archbishop replied on June 14th to say that Perugino had left Venice. Unable to secure his services himself at that time, the Duke recommended Perugino to the monks of the Certosa at Pavia, and commissioned a great altar-piece from him. Accordingly, in October 1496, we hear of Perugino being at Pavia working at the altar-piece. In the following year, 1497, Il Moro again tried to secure the services of Perugino for the Castello, and wrote to one of the Baglioni, who at that time ruled over Perugia, begging him to send Perugino to him; but the artist was then at work in Perugia, and so full of commissions that he declined Il Moro's offer, and never went to the Castello.

The two years, 1494 and 1495, saw the completion of the altar-piece for the Magistrates' Chapel in Perugia – now in the Vatican Gallery and already mentioned, – the great "Entombment" in the Pitti Palace, the "Ascension" altar-piece for San Pietro, Perugia, the portrait of Francesco delle Opere in the Uffizi, and the commencement of the greatest work of all, which was finished in 1496, the "Crucifixion" at Sta. Maria Maddalena dei Pazzi.

The "Ascension" altar-piece is the first one that we have to consider of that group of Perugino's altar-pieces which have been divided, the component parts being scattered throughout Europe. To this division and scattering fuller attention is given in the next chapter, and it will suffice here to state that the centre part is at Lyons, the lunette at St. Gervais, Paris, the predella in three panels at Rouen, and the surrounding saints divided, three in the Vatican Gallery and five in the church of S. Pietro, where at one time the complete work rested. The picture at Borgo San Sepolcro is usually spoken of as a replica of the centre piece of this great picture, but I am strongly disposed to take an opposite view of the case.

Vasari records the painting of the Borgo picture, which was, he says, "executed for the Abbot Simone de' Graziani and transported to the church of San Gilio at Borgo on the backs of porters at very heavy cost." He also records the painting of the picture for S. Pietro, naming it almost at the close of his biographical notes on the artist; and of this picture he says: "The whole of it is replete with evidences of thought and care, insomuch that it is one of the best paintings in oil executed by Pietro in Perugia." It is quite impossible to accept the chronology Vasari gives, as he mixes up dates in the most hopeless confusion; but in this instance I think he is right in putting the Borgo picture before the Lyons one rather than *vice versâ*.

The picture at Borgo is in bad condition: the one at Lyons has been transferred to canvas and very much repainted, and still shows signs of two vertical splits in the panel; but, despite all these injuries, the Borgo picture is, I consider, the finer of the two, and the Lyons one, although by the same hand, a later and more careless replica.

In the Borgo picture the Virgin is in religious garb and has the head covered: in the Lyons picture there is a more secular garb, the head uncovered and short hair to be seen. In the Borgo picture the angels carry loosely looped narrow ribbon carefully and gracefully drawn: the ribbon in the Lyons picture is broader, more coarsely painted, lettered throughout, and falling in awkward folds. The wings of the cherubs in the mandorla at Borgo are painted with exquisite detail, every little scale and feather being carefully represented; these details are almost entirely absent in the Lyons picture, where the wings of the cherubs appear to be hurriedly painted and lacking altogether in finish. There is far greater sweetness in the faces at Borgo, especially those of the Redeemer, the Virgin, St. Peter, and St. Paul, than at Lyons, where all these four important faces are roughly and even coarsely delineated. In some of the attendant disciples, the hair, which at Borgo is daintily painted in, and flows in slightly ringletted form, hangs loosely at Lyons and is of a harsher texture, and the wonderful trees sharply delineated against the sky and full of exquisite foliage at Borgo, are hardly to be seen at Lyons, and are represented by half-a-dozen dwarfish shrubs.

The mandorla in the Borgo picture is a deep luminous band of mysterious colour, out of which, and against the light fleecy clouds, rise the cherub faces: at Lyons it is a flat band of heavy colour, the clouds are woolly and thick, and the cherub faces, instead of rising from the wondrous depth, lay superimposed upon the mandorla as upon a piece of board.

I am strongly of opinion that the Borgo picture was the original work, the Lyons one, for which he contracted to the monks of Cassino, March 6th, 1495, being either a somewhat hurried replica of it in which the master grew tired of the monotony of repetition, or else that it was a picture in which a certain amount of labour was left to assistants and pupils. There is an important study for three apostles, in the Uffizi, which was clearly prepared for the Borgo picture and not for the Lyons one, as, while closely resembling the former, it differs from the latter in one or two important details. This is not the accepted theory, I know, and it is one that will probably not meet with universal acceptance, but a careful comparison of the pictures leads me to a clear opinion in the matter. With regard to the pilaster saints the case is different. Those at the Vatican are all genuine work of the master and are extremely fine, and the same may be said of three of the five at Perugia, but two of them are not entirely Perugino's work, and bear traces of a pupil's hand. The three predella pictures on the other hand, which are at Rouen, are charming examples of the master's work, and are bathed in that wonderful golden sunlight which is so distinctive of his finest work. In each picture a strip of the foreground which was damaged in transit has had to be restored: in the "Adoration" it is the very slightest bit along the front of the whole picture; in the "Resurrection" it is a wider piece, embracing part of the feet of three of the sleeping soldiers and the edge of the stone slab on which the tomb rests; but in the third picture, the "Baptism," the damage is serious, as the foreground strip includes the feet of Our Lord and one foot of the Baptist. In all other respects these three panels are exquisite specimens of Perugino's fine and discriminative work.

With respect to the lunette it must be noted that Crowe and Cavalcaselle and many other writers are in error in stating that it hangs in St. Germain l'Auxerrois in Paris, whereas it is in St. Gervais, a very different church. It is not in good condition, having suffered much from cleaning and repair, and it has a horizontal split which nearly divides it into two pieces. It is nevertheless clearly discernible as a fine work from the master's hand. There is neither predella nor lunette at Borgo S. Sepolcro. There is no question as to the date of the S. Pietro altar-piece, as the original contract for painting it is still in existence and appears in full in Orsini. [*L] It is dated 8th March 1496, and recites how the abbot and chapter of the monastery gave out on contract to Perugino the picture of the High Altar for the price of 500 gold ducats. The Borgo picture was therefore, I contend, a little earlier, but perhaps only a year in advance of the other. The picture of Francesco delle Opere belongs to this same period, but as in the chapter on the Cambio it will be further discussed, it may well be passed with brief mention at this place. Finally, as part of the work of these two prolific years, comes one of our artist's masterpieces, the "Entombment," now in the Pitti Palace. Space composition is seen in this picture in its full vigour. How quiet is the atmosphere of the scene, how reverent and tender a mood it creates. How vast is the space in which the episode is placed, and how marvellously is the sense of immeasurable distance produced.

The picture is one of the most beautiful that Perugino ever painted. The composition is very clever, well balanced and well grouped, while the faces are of a serene beauty that was never surpassed in later works. It is well to notice that the dead body of

Our Lord retains much of the flexibility of life, while quite as clearly is seen the weight and the looseness of death. The mourners around are full of tender pity, while the grief of the Virgin is too great for words, and evinces itself in the look of deep affection that fills that wonderful face. Each figure is, however, distinct, self-centred, and enfolded in its own grief. It is only the fact that each one is thinking of the great central figure that gives to the picture, as a whole, any real completeness. It is a sober, thoughtful composition, full of sentiment, but lacking any of the strong moving force that other schools gave to a similar representation, and, although the forerunner of Fra Bartolommeo's greater work, it has none of the intensity that his more emotional nature could present.

Some delightful studies for this picture appear in the Uffizi, marked by most careful study. The clenched hands of one of the two persons who stand close to Nicodemus are very noteworthy. The action is so expressive of intense, but restrained sorrow, and the drawing of the fine, delicate, but muscular hands, is particularly excellent. In the studies the richly-ornamented cap of the youth in the group does not appear. The cap in the drawing is quite plain, and the face, which in the picture is very expressive, is hard and uninteresting. Another large pen drawing for this picture exists, and is in Christ Church, Oxford. By some critics it is not accepted as a work of Perugino's. It is ascribed to one of his pupils, or to a later man altogether, especially because several of the faces are hard and unimpressive. Let, however, the drapery be closely examined, and the curious formation with dark hollows and oval curves will be recognised at once. The large projecting great toe, and the manner in which it sets away from the other toes, leaving a clear space between it and them, is noticeable, while the limp flexibility of the bare flesh of the Christ is also an important criterion in deciding on the origin of the drawing. To me it appears as a thoroughly genuine work, marking out the general grouping of the picture. The positions of Nicodemus, Mary Cleophas, and the youth, underwent some slight changes, and the other figures near to Nicodemus were introduced, but the picture preserves very closely the original suggestions of the drawing.

The finished picture was executed for the nuns of Santa Chiara, but when they had obtained it, so highly was it admired, that Vasari records that a rich Florentine, Francesco del Pugliese, offered them three times the price that they had paid for it, as well as a replica from the master's own hand, but the tempting offer was declined, as Pietro had told them that he did not think he could equal the one they possessed.

CHAPTER V

THE STORY OF THE PILLAGE

There are two noteworthy circumstances that affect the biographer of Perugino. On the one hand is the fact that so many of his pictures are dated, and hence along the story of his life stand out clearly defined certain pieces of definite evidence, marking his progress and his years. On the other hand is the opposing circumstance that most of his altar-pieces have been taken to pieces, removed from their original home, and scattered in all directions throughout Europe, so much so that the task of reconstructing the most important, that of S. Agostino, is one of serious difficulty.

This scattering has enormously increased the troubles of the biographer, obliging him to journey from Paris to Marseilles, from Grenoble to Bordeaux, from Strassburg to Tarbes in order to inspect all the parts of even one picture, and even in Perugia itself renders it almost impossible to speak definitely of the history of certain altar-pieces.

It is from the French occupation of Italy that all these difficulties result. There was a time prior to 1796 when Perugia was very rich with the works of her adopted son Pietro Perugino. At that time almost every church possessed pictures by the master; the altar-piece painted in 1495 for the magistrates' chapel was still *in situ,* and the public buildings in the city were possessed of rich decoration, the work of that artist whom Perugia had delighted to honour and employ.

After the armistice of Bologna had been signed in 1796, French commissioners were sent through Italy to demand and select pictures and other works of art which Napoleon required as spoil from his defeated enemies.

Perugia, as a city rich in art treasures, suffered greatly. The treaty of Tolentino (1797) demanded urgency, and, without any delay, a commissioner, Tinet by name, descended upon Perugia, and, on the very day on which the treaty was signed, addressed a letter to the Priori, demanding in the name of the Republic leave of entry into all churches, monasteries, and public places, in order to select such objects as he thought were worthy of transmission to Paris. He did not confine himself to an arrangement that had been made in the previous July, that Perugia was to furnish three pictures as its ransom, but demanded free right to take what he pleased. His orders were too pressing to be eluded, and the Priori had no course but to obey. The pillage commenced on the 20th, and lasted for two days, but Tinet was not satisfied. He had a strong impression that many of the best things were hidden from him, and so in even more emphatic terms he demanded that the superiors of St. Augustine and St. Antoine, and the librarians of the religious orders and of the town should give him access in order that he might select their greatest treasures and whatever he thought worthy of adorning the museums of the great republic. Meantime, secretly by night, with urgent haste, the treasures of the religious houses were being hidden away. The altar-pieces were divided and the smaller portions, pictures from the predelle, and panels of attendant saints were carried to private houses, hidden under floors and behind panelling, and secreted in every possible way. Reliquaries and monstrances were in wells, and railings and iron grilles covered over with grease and dirt in order to hide them from the covetous gaze of the commissioner.

Tinet was, however, unfortunately, a very determined man, and a connoisseur to boot, and in the two days' search, he had obtained the chief treasures in Perugia. It appeared at one time as though that notable picture, the altar-piece in the Magistrates' Chapel, painted in 1495, would be overlooked, but he remembered it at the very last moment and it was included. To add insult to injury, the Perugians were ordered to pack and transmit their treasures, but every possible effort was made to delay the work and prevent their being sent off. Much correspondence ensued, and the Priori did their utmost to raise difficulties, but all was to no purpose, and on March 27th six carriages drawn by twenty-four oxen and attended by six peasants, quitted Perugia amid the tears and lamentations of the people, carrying with them the greatest treasures of the city, never to be seen again within its walls. The very magnificent proportions of many of Perugino's pictures rendered it impossible for them to be concealed, their predella pictures and pilaster saints were in some instances safe, but the central panels it was impossible to guard, and in the thirty-two pictures carried off to Paris, there were included twelve of the greatest of the master's works, and also the famous "Sposalizio" from the chapel of the Anello, and the "Palladium" of the city, the altar-piece from the Magistrates' Chapel. Drawn by the great white Umbrian oxen, and slowly journeying across Europe, these heavily-laden vans took their way, and the pictures that for three hundred years had been objects of devotion and delight to the good people of Perugia, and were cruelly torn from their resting places, went to swell the vanity of the terrible conqueror in Paris.

Still, however, Perugia now so poor in her master's works, was too rich for envious eyes. The peace of Vienna had been signed, there was a pause in the warfare in Europe prior to the invasion of Russia in 1812, and some attention was given to internal affairs. On the 25th of February 1811 appeared an Imperial decree, requiring that the treasures in the department of the Trasimène (as the district under its new French rulers was styled) should be brought together in order to ornament the picture galleries that Napoleon had erected. With cruel irony the decree stated that, doubtless, the people of Perugia would rejoice that their pictures were deemed worthy to ornament the galleries of Paris.

Napoleon himself had a great admiration for the works of Perugino, and the pictures he owned by the master made him desirous of possessing more; and as with the conqueror to desire was to obtain, he immediately issued this decree regardless of the feelings of his newly conquered subjects. The Count de Champagny, who was the minister charged with the execution of the decree, passed on to Count Daru, his subordinate in the "French" city of Rome, a list of pictures that had been prepared by Baron Denon, the director of the gallery, who had passed his youth in Italy, and being a great connoisseur, had an excellent memory of what fine Italian pictures were left in the plundered city.

Count Daru was to pass on the list to Baron Roederer, Prefect of the Trasimène, who on his part was to see that the Sub-Prefect Spada gave every assistance to one, Tofanelli, who was to select and transmit the pictures.

Tofanelli arrived in Perugia September 30th, 1812, and one day sufficed for him to make his selection. Forty-eight pictures were selected, and packed in cases ready for transmission, an agreement entered into between him and the town, signed by himself and countersigned by the mayor, and a contract sealed between him and Signor Franceschini for removing the pictures to Rome, and then Tofanelli hurried off back to Rome. The pictures were to be sent immediately, but upon Tofanelli's departure, a long series of delays and negotiations commenced, suggested and arranged by the mayor in order to save the pictures. This worthy man, Cesarei, deserves better recognition to-day in Perugia. He worked valiantly for the city, and now his name is nearly forgotten. While Tofanelli was in Perugia, he dissembled his feelings, aided the commissioner, signed any papers that were presented to him, had the pictures packed, and gaily saluted Tofanelli as he left the city; but once the commissioner had gone, he determined to do his very utmost to prevent the forty-eight pictures gathered from the shrines of his city leaving its gates. He appealed to the bishop and to the government, he worried the prefect and the sub-prefect, and eventually obtained a promise that those pictures which were specially dear as objects before which the Perugians paid their devotions might be retained. Forthwith the cases were opened, and these pictures replaced in their original positions, to the great joy of the people.

Hardly had this been done than the permission was countermanded. The mayor was regretting that he had asked for so little, and that the pictures in the sacristies and corridors of the monasteries would not be grouped with those taken from the churches. He was explaining that all the pictures were equally dear to the Perugians, when again an order arrived to send on all the pictures. Once more the mayor dissembled. He promised to send the cases as soon as he could obtain carriages, but at the same time wrote, to the Count Daru, to the Director of the Police in Rome, and to the Count Baglioni Oddi, one of the deputies in Paris, invoking the interests of religion and of art of the province and of the capital to save his beloved pictures. Again he won a temporary success. On August 26th an order arrived from headquarters, permitting Perugia to retain twenty out of the forty-eight pictures chosen by Tofanelli. Once more there was rejoicing, but again came disaster. Count Daru intervened, every concession was overturned, and a fresh order from even higher authorities reached the mayor, ordering him to send on without delay to the Capitol at Rome, every picture selected by Tofanelli. These instructions the mayor stated he could not understand. He wrote on November 16, stating that, of course, this last order did not include the pictures just given back to Perugia, and appealing to Baron Roederer for consideration, adding as a reason that he could not be responsible for the people should the pictures that they cherished be taken away.

To this appeal Roederer turned a deaf ear. He wrote on December 4, again on December 8, and again on December 13, stating that it was impossible to admit any reasons, and he must demand that all the pictures be sent at once. The mayor, indefatigable as ever, wrote again and again, raised all kinds of difficulties, continued to warn the authorities that the people would make a tumult, and that he could not be responsible for their tranquillity, and finally sent letters from the clergy of San Severo and San Costanzo supporting his statements.

All was of no avail. On November 6th, 1813, final definite orders arrived, and the precious cases had to be sent to Rome.

A few more days' delay would have saved the pictures, as at the moment that the cases reached Rome the Neapolitans under Murat entered the city, and French dominion in Rome was at an end. Even then the irony of circumstance continued, for, when, on January 6th, 1814, the pictures arrived in Paris, the allied forces arrived also, and Baron Denon was ordered to restore to their lawful proprietors the pictures that had been stolen.

The most unfortunate part of the story has now to be told. Instead of forcing France to restore the booty at her own cost and at once, the allies, in more merciful mood, simply demanded that she should send for the Italian representatives and permit them to take away their property. Only ten days were allowed in Paris for the booty to be secured, packed, and transmitted, and, as envoys arrived from all parts of Italy, and each was eager to obtain what he could as quickly as possible, very many pictures were left behind. The pictures sent to Paris in 1797 had been more in number than could be accommodated in the gallery, and, as it is so easy to give away other people's property, the government had distributed as marks of favour and bribes for tranquillity many of the best Italian pictures amongst the provincial museums in France. Many of these pictures Canova, who was sent by the Holy See, failed to trace; others it was impossible to obtain, as, although the allies were in possession of Paris, they were not equally masters of the distant provinces in France, and, consequently, in France these pictures remained. Even of those twenty-one pictures stolen from Perugia in 1812 but two were returned to Italy, and those only got as far as Rome.

Englishmen may well feel proud of their part in this transaction. It was the firmness of the British Government [*M] that enabled the Vatican Gallery to take its position as one of the great picture galleries of the world. They not only enforced the restitution by the French of the plunder accumulated in the Louvre by the rapacious arms of Napoleon, but even contributed some £30,000 to defray the expenses of the removal, which the finances of Pius VII. could ill afford, no other allied power contributing one farthing.

Canova gathered up, in the short time at his disposal, and with the limited means that he possessed, all the fine pictures that he could obtain, and the treasures now in Rome are the proof of his zeal and exertions.

Meantime the Priori of Perugia waited for two years, hoping against hope that their treasures might come back to them. At length, in September 1816, they wrote to Canova, and he replied to them on the 20th. His letter explained how encompassed with difficulty he had been in Paris, how short a time had been allowed him in which to remove the pictures, how small were the means at his disposal, how scattered were the pictures, and how impossible it was, without force of arms to travel from department to department and take possession of the property.

With regard to one notable picture about which the Perugians were specially anxious, the "Ascension," from San Pietro, he explained that the people of Lyons had appealed to the Pope for permission to retain it. They set forth their attachment to the Holy See, their zeal for the Chief Pontiff, and the singular affection which they had manifested toward His Holiness whenever he passed by Lyons. Their petition received attention, and the cardinal secretary wrote, on November 13th, 1816, an authoris-ation to the city of Lyons to retain the picture which had been so disgracefully torn from its resting-place in Perugia.

Canova was evidently as anxious as were the Perugians to obtain back all the pictures; but events were too strong for him, and the poor Perugians never again possessed the great treasures of art which, prior to 1797, made their city one of the richest in Italy.

Cesarei, the indefatigable mayor of Perugia, who had been appointed *gonfaloniere* year after year in order to obtain restitution of the pictures, did not give up hope of obtaining his end for some years. He tried hard to obtain the two pictures which English generosity had restored to Italy, and he worried the Holy See with repeated letters and appeals.

At length Cardinal Consalvi, on October 8th, 1817, closed the whole episode by a letter to Cesarei. He explained that the pictures were all presented by the allied forces to the Sovereign Pontiff as the Head of the Pontifical states from which they had been taken, and that they were exposed in Rome for the education of the students who came from all over Europe to study in the Queen of Cities. In consequence, the Papal Government had the right, the Cardinal continued, to retain the pictures.

It may be added that, even if the Holy See had not the right to retain the pictures, it had too much business on hand at that time to be able to give attention to works of art, and insufficient money in its depleted treasury to pay for their removal.

Such is the story, with all its mournful details, of the pillage of Perugia, and it will now be easily understood why the provincial museums of France are so rich in the works of this master.

To reconstruct the great altar-piece of St. Agostino means that visits must be made to Lyons, Grenoble, Toulouse, Nantes, and Perugia. For another altar-piece it is necessary to visit Rouen, Lyons, Perugia, Rome, and Paris; while yet other pictures are at Caen, Nancy, Tarbes, Bordeaux, Strassburg, Marseilles, Lille, and Chantilly.

The scattering is not now wholly confined to France, for pictures at one time in France are now at Altenburg, Frankfort,

Vienna, and St. Petersburg, while odd pieces of these self-same pictures remain to-day in Perugia.

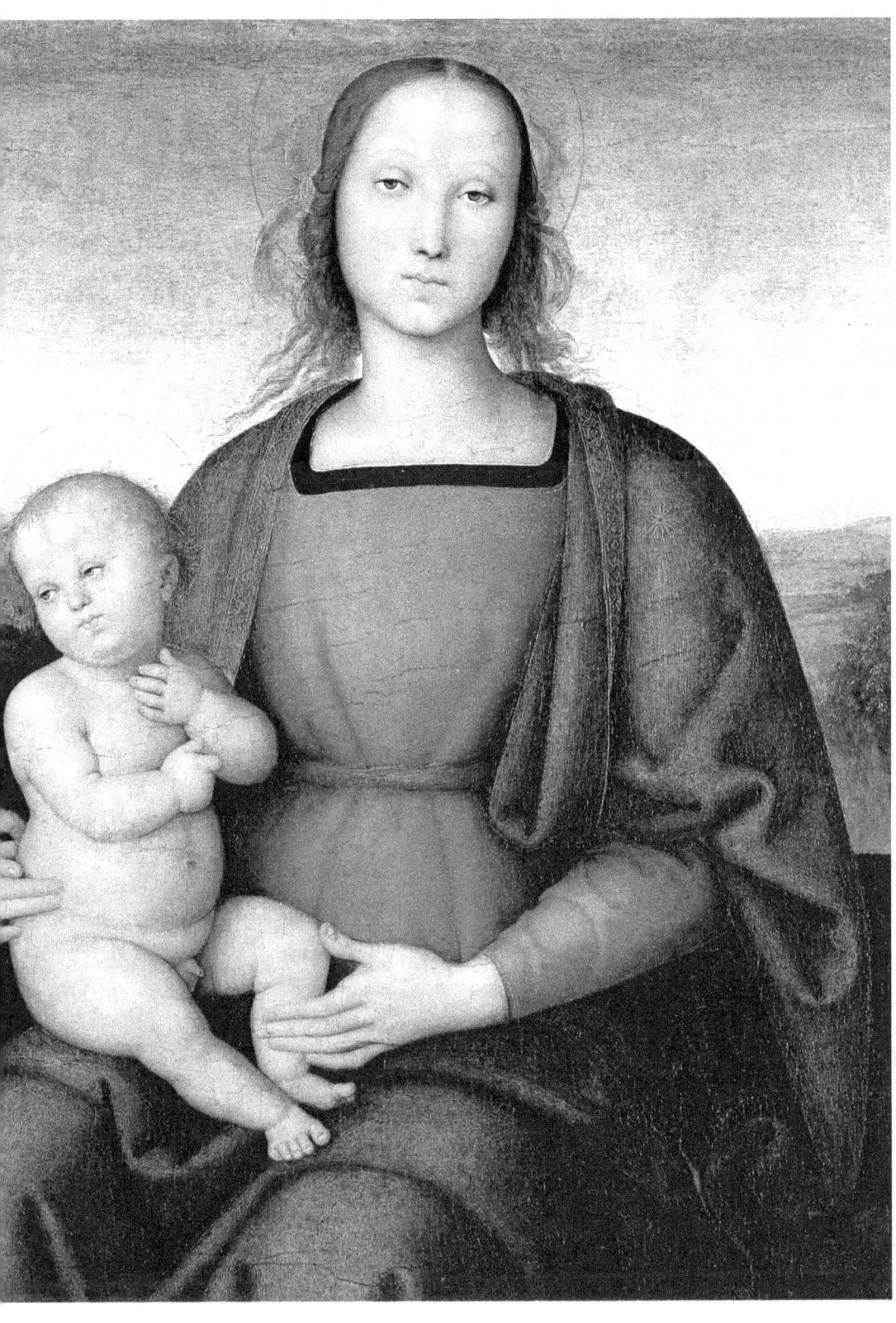

Perugino, Madonna and Child, 1500

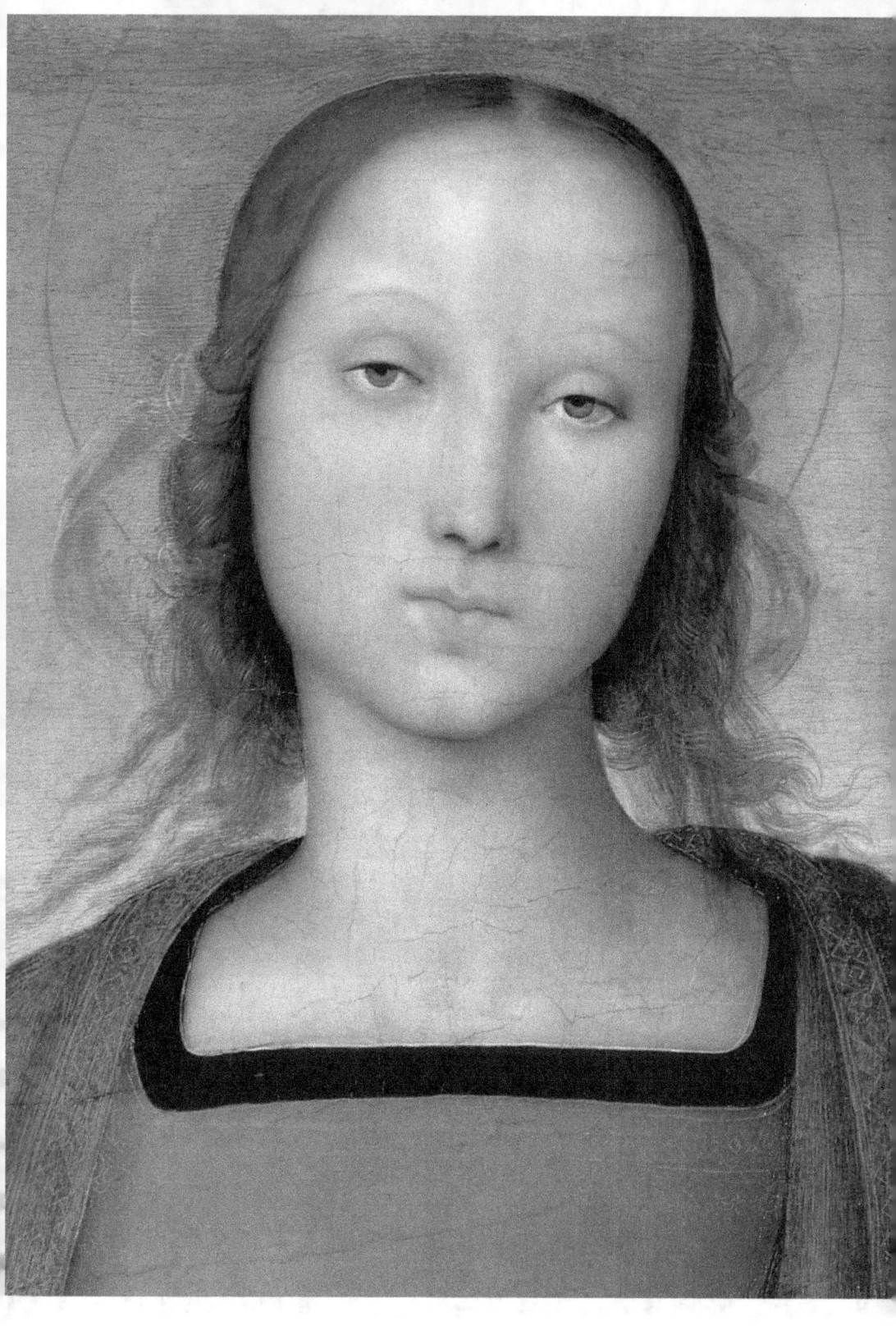

Perugino, Madonna and Child, 1500, detail

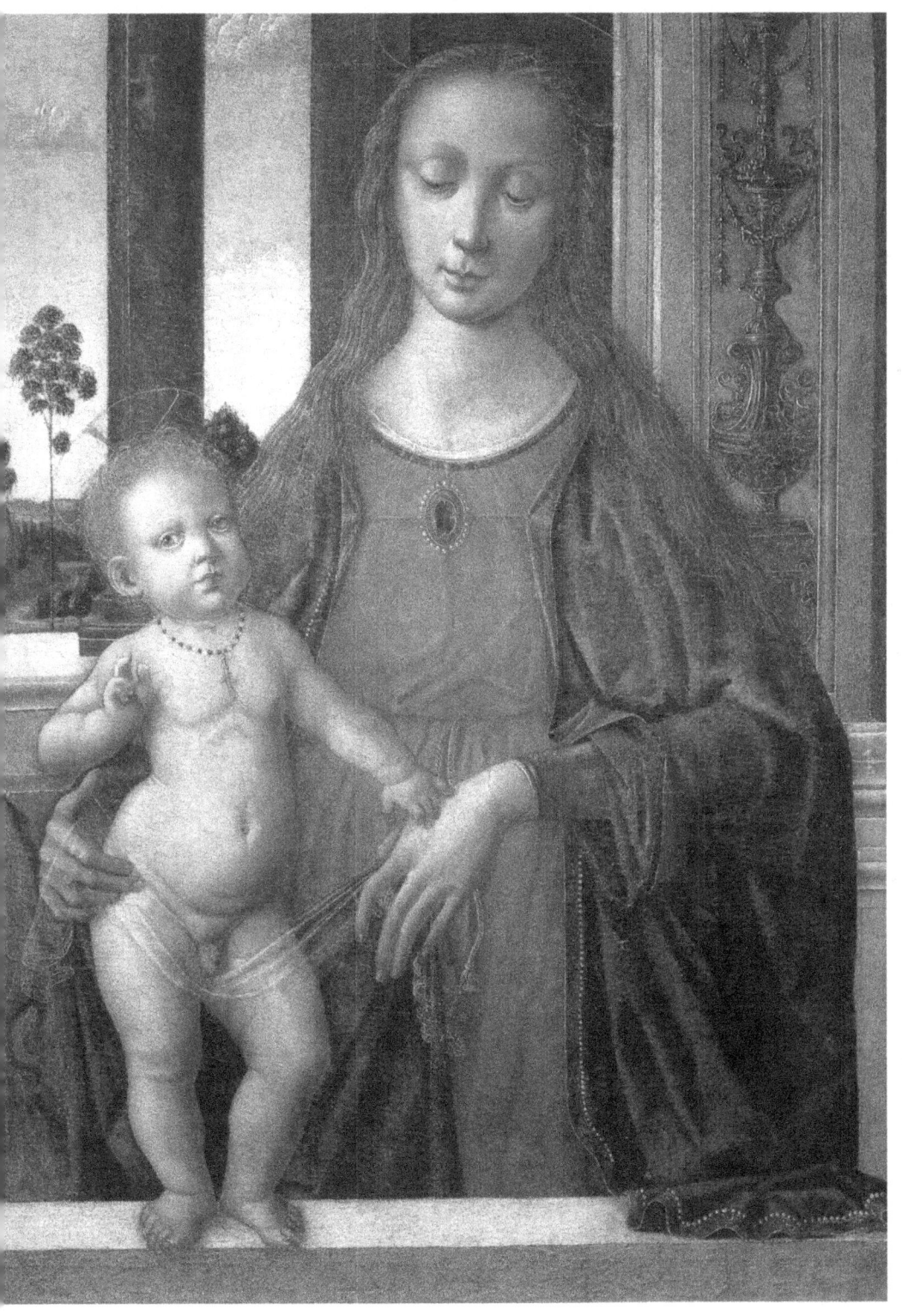

Perugino, Madonna and Child, 1470-73

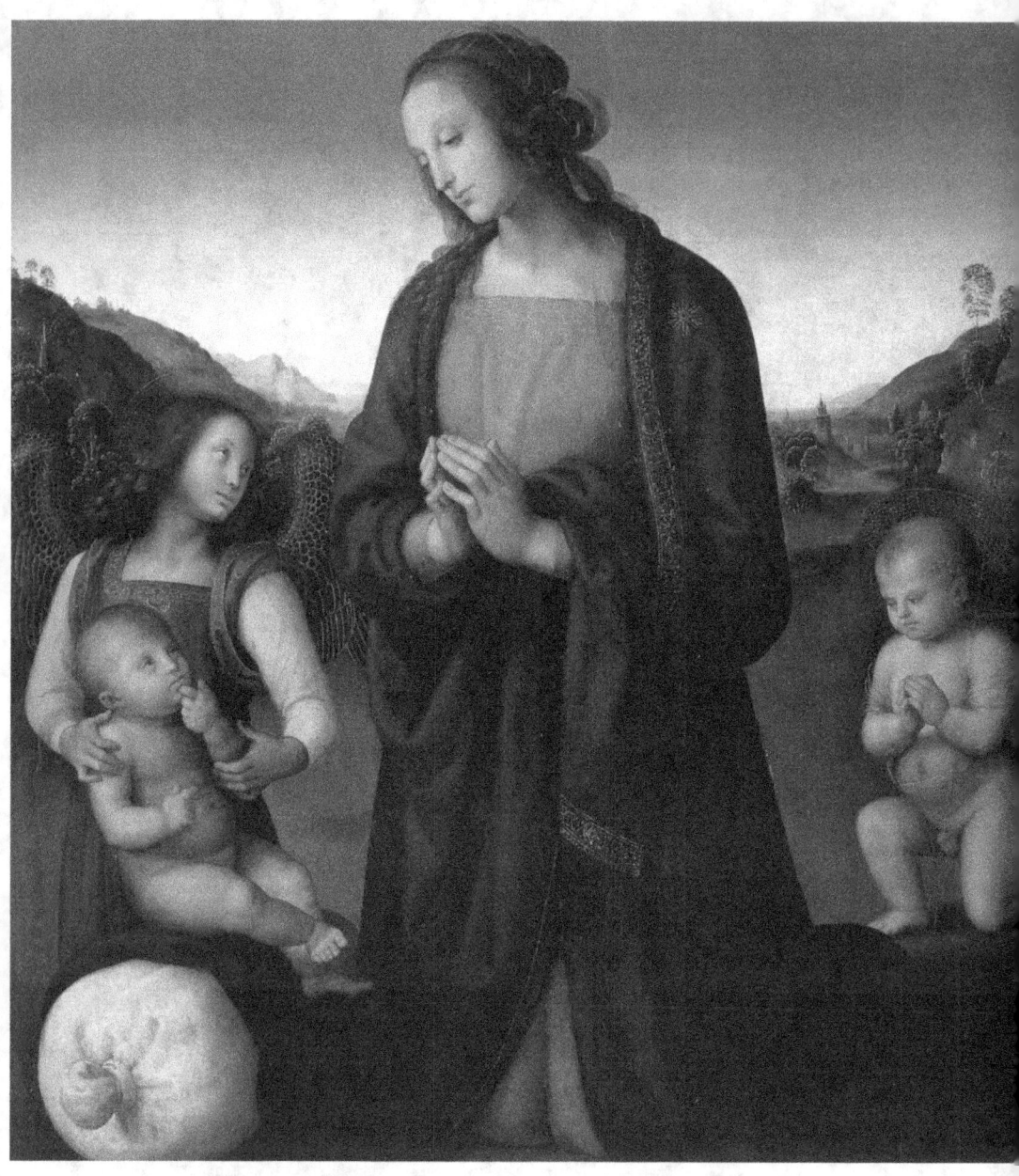

Perugino, Madonna and Child, 1445-48,
Pitti Palace

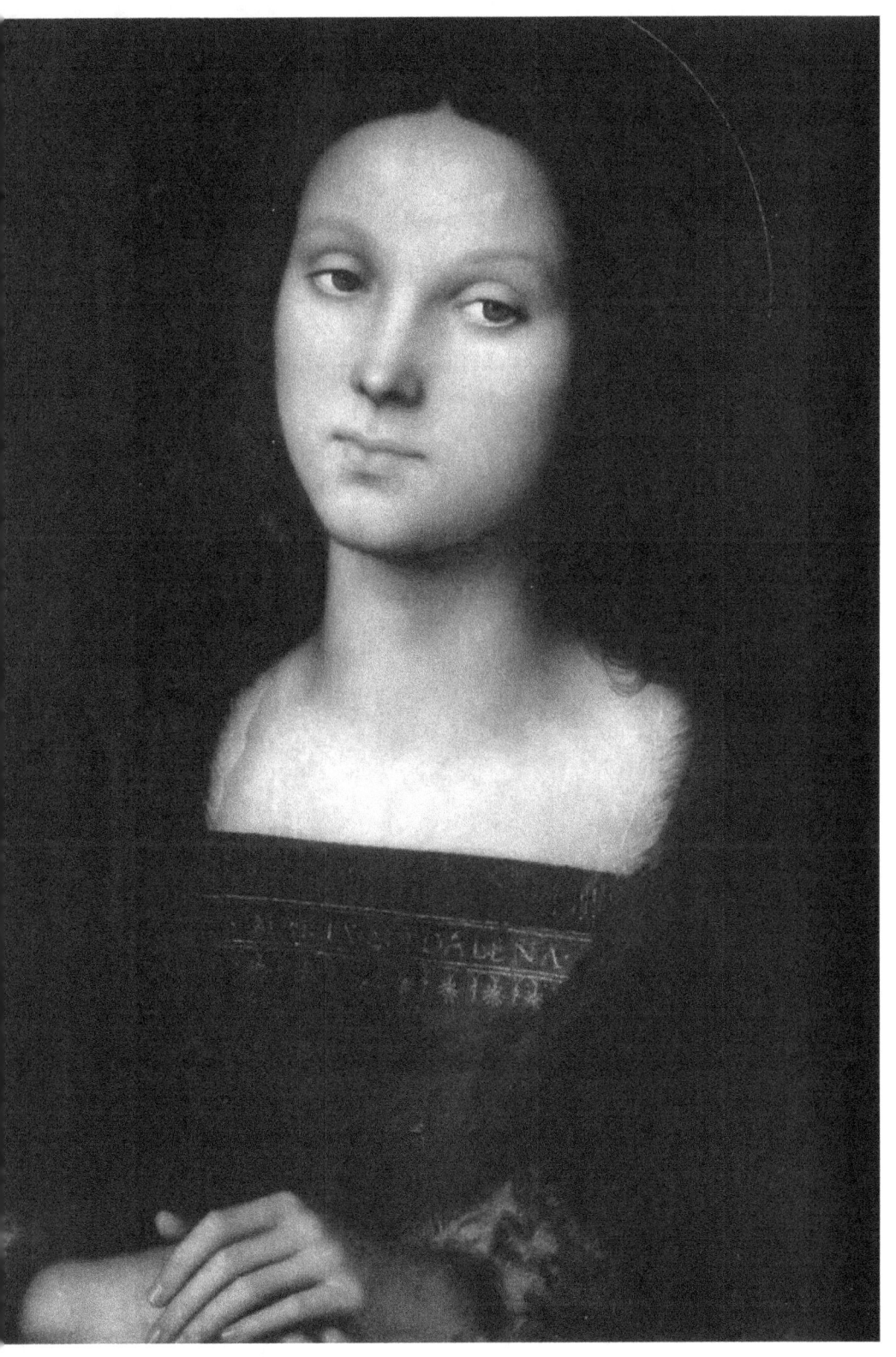

Perugino, Mary Magdalene, 1445-48

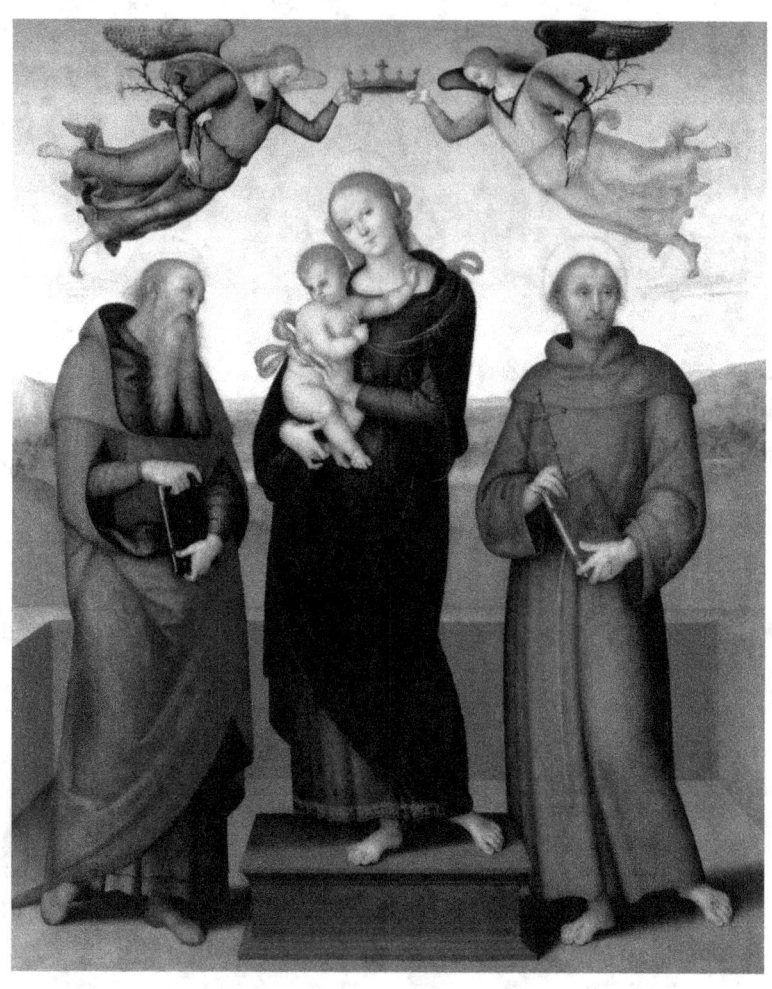

Perugino, Virgin and Child With Saints, 1507,
National Gallery, London

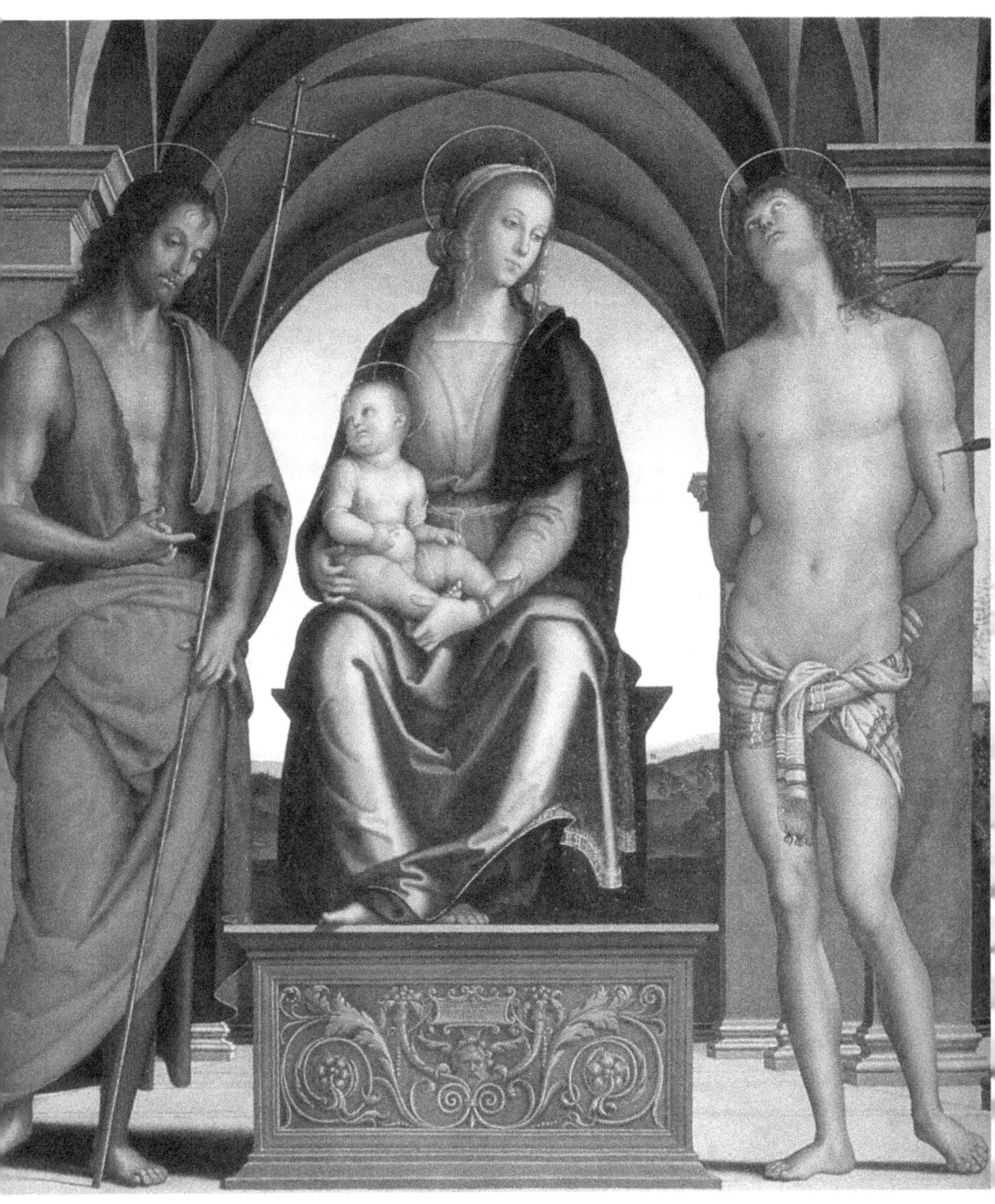

Perugino, The Madonna, Child and Saints,
1493, Uffizi

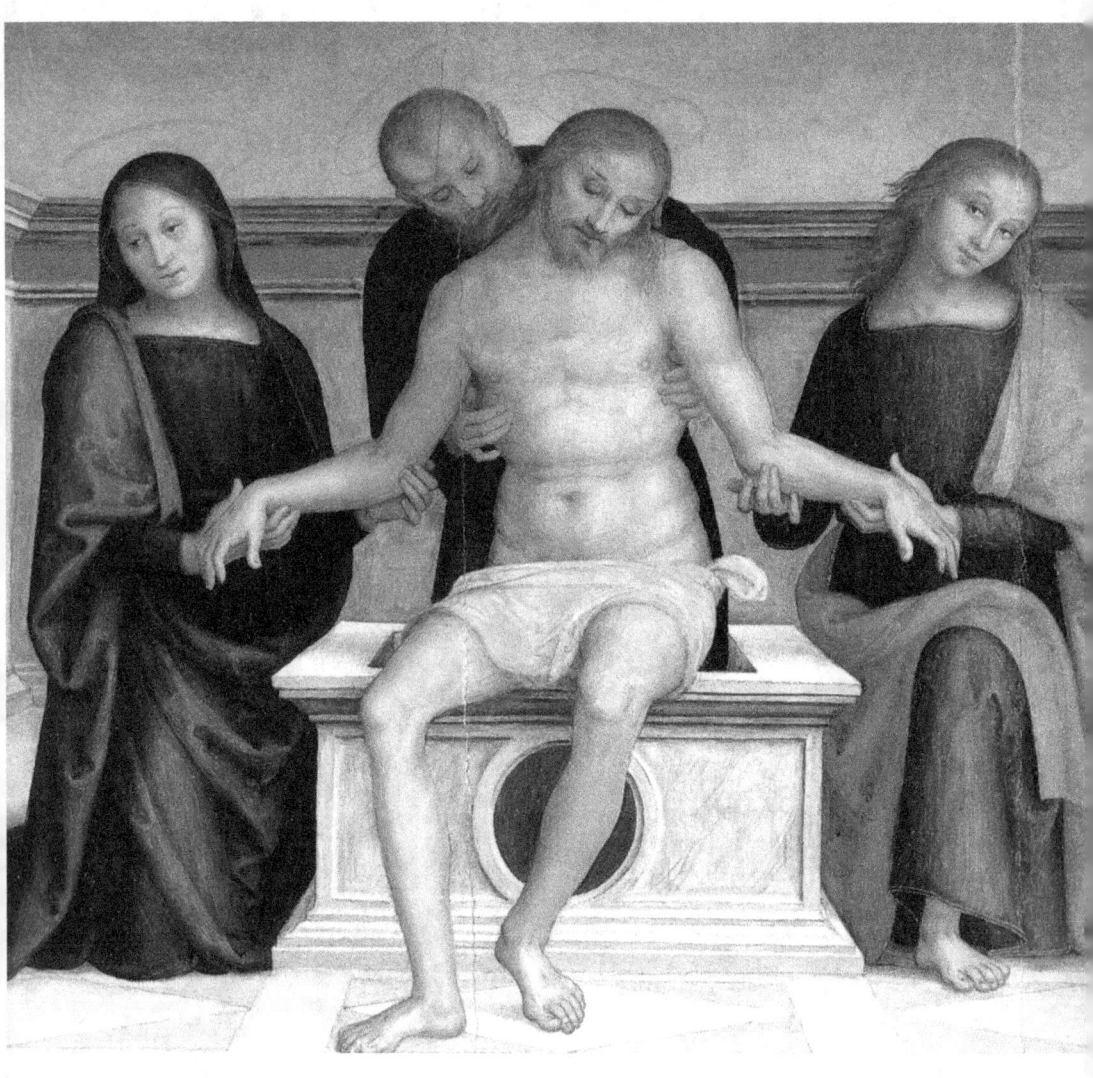

Perugino, The Dead Christ, 1512-13

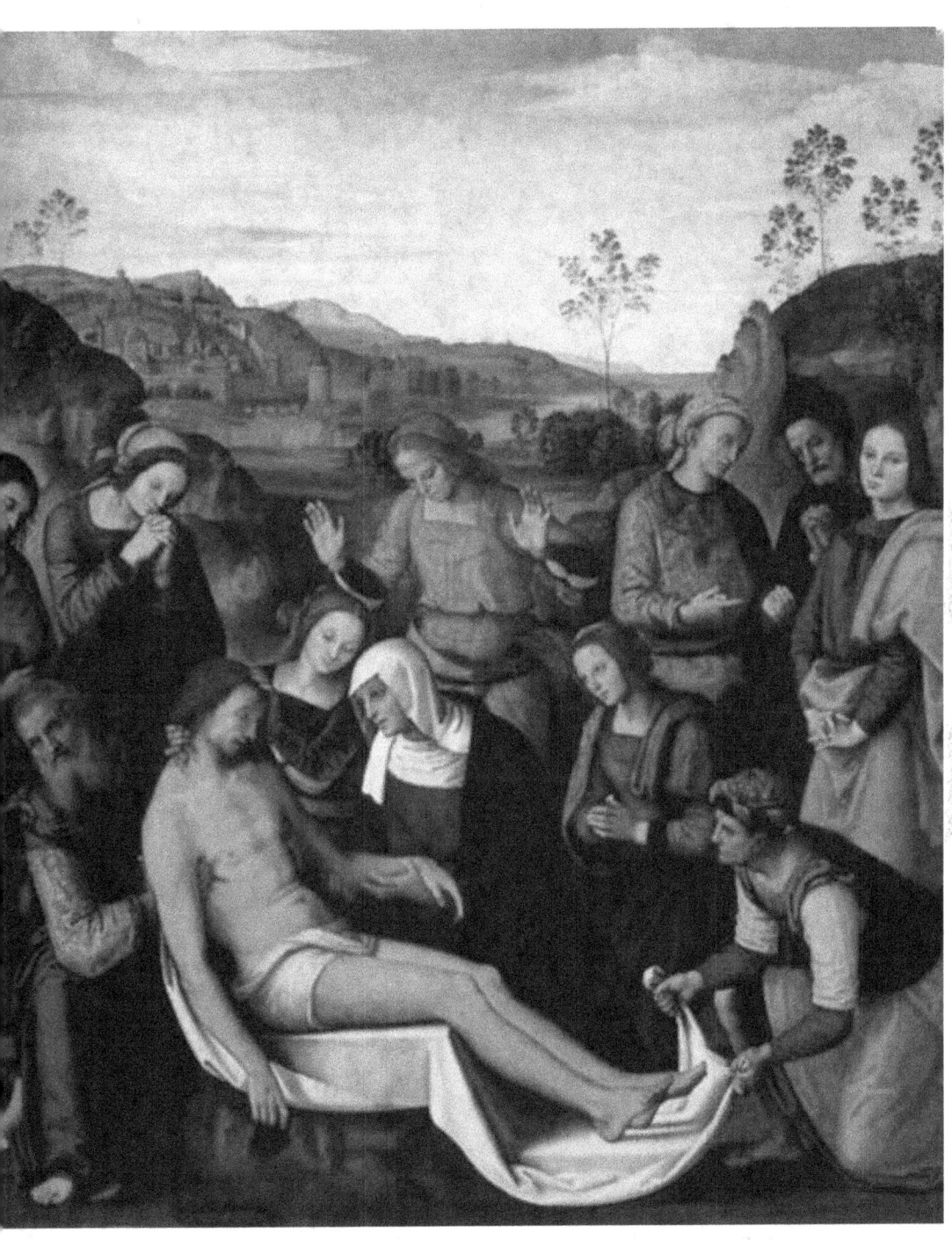

Perugino, The Mourning of the Dead Christ, 1495

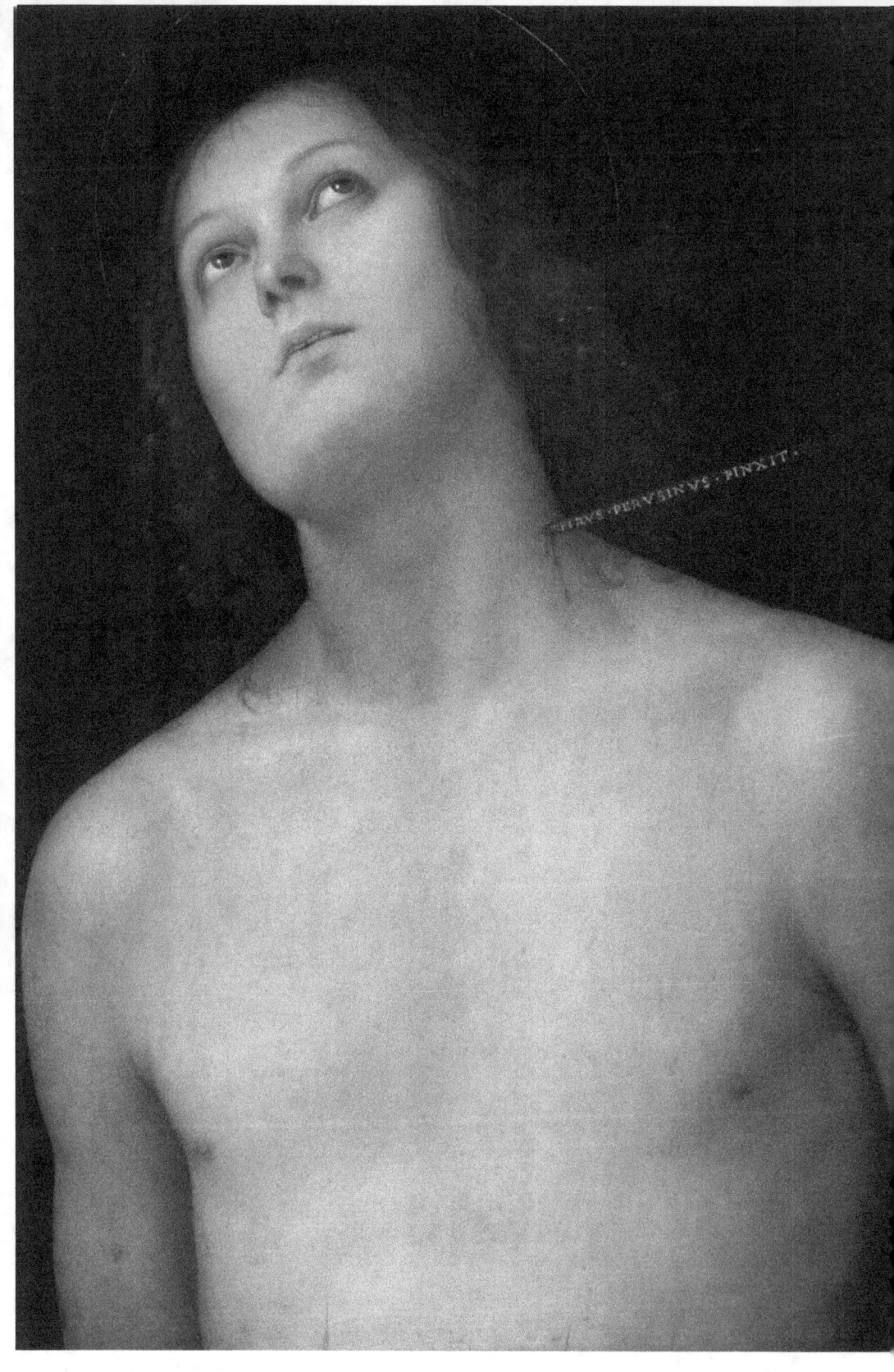

Perugino, St Sebastian, 1475-78

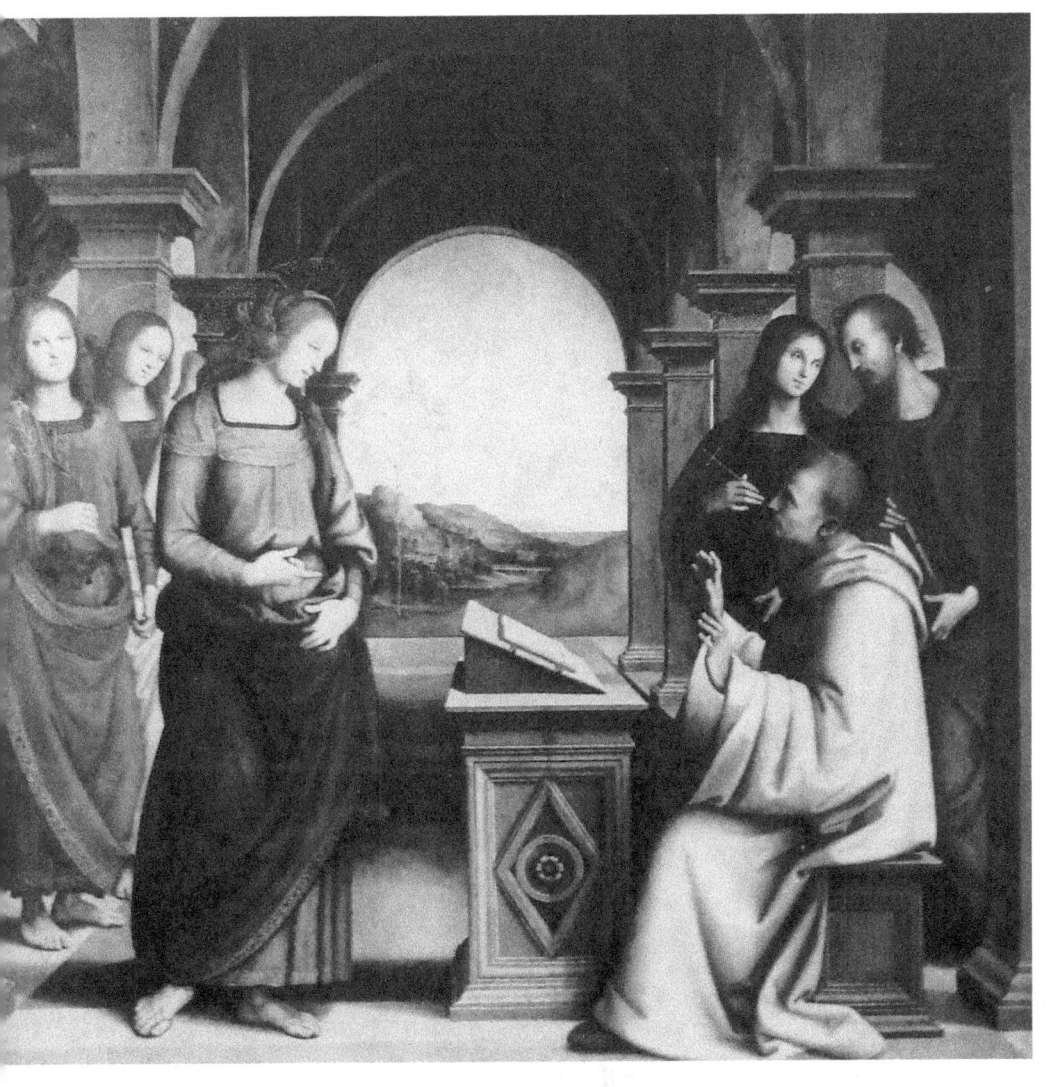

Perugino, Vision of St Bernard, 1488

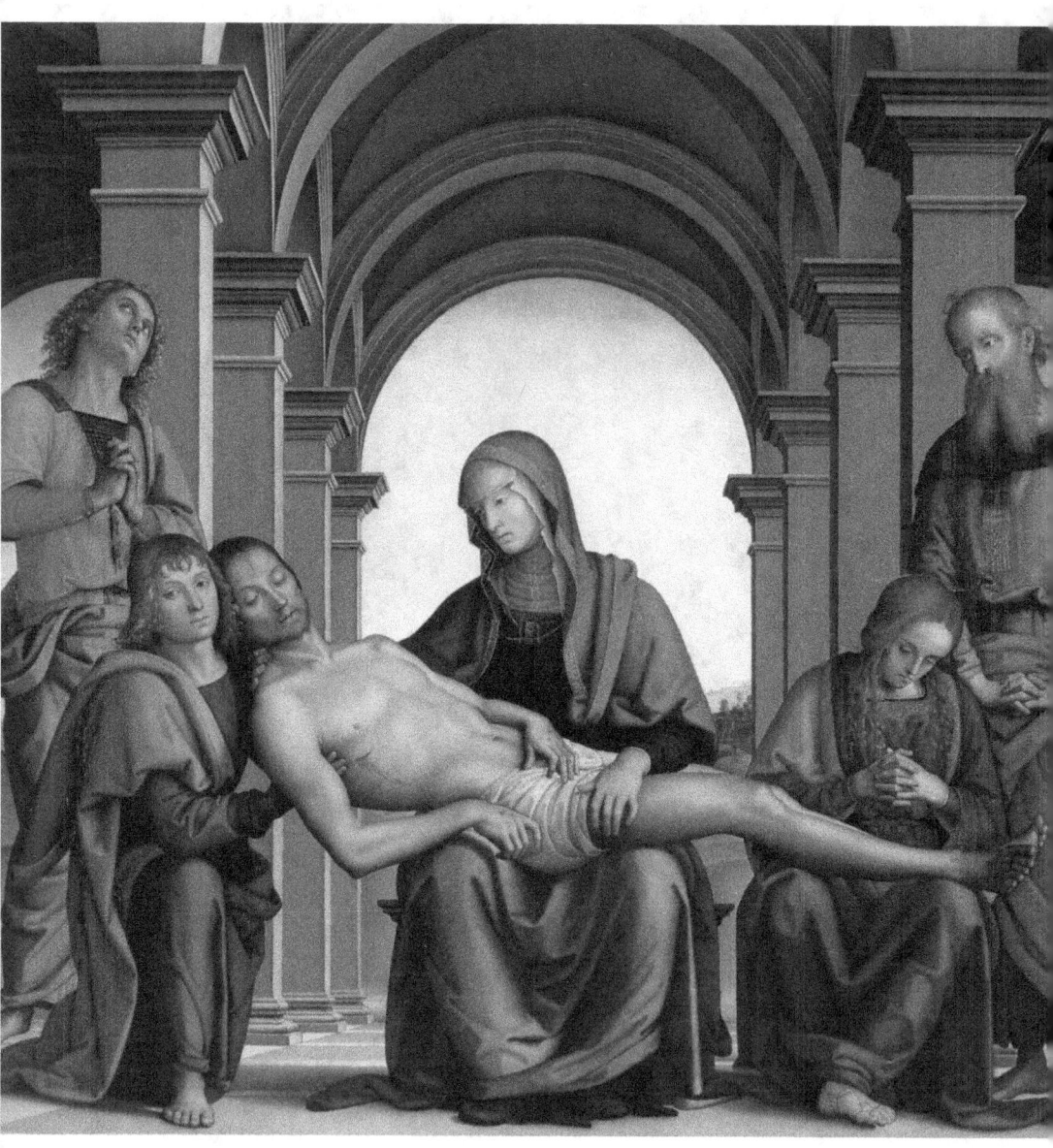

Perugino, Pietà, 1490, Uffizi

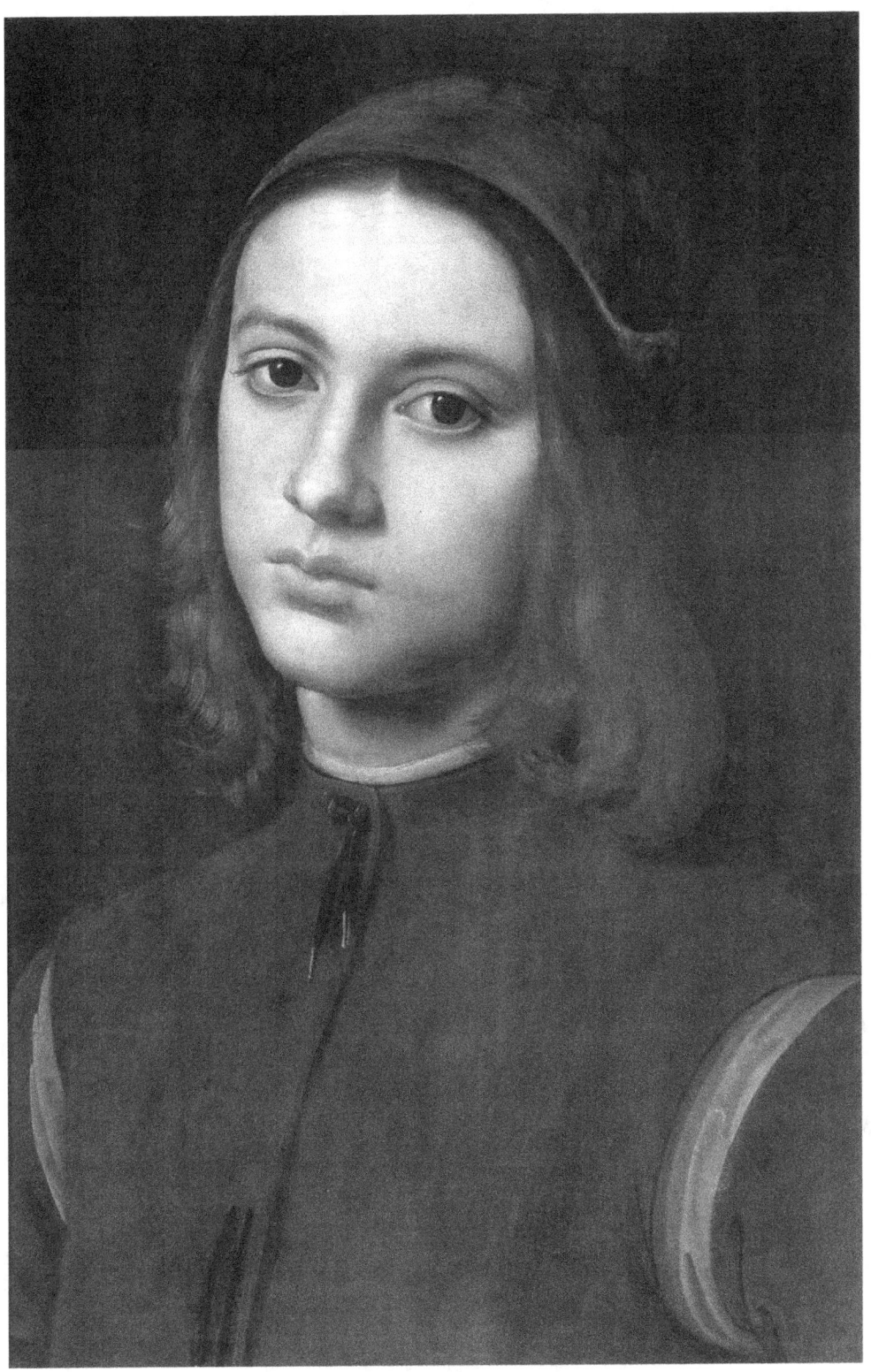

Perugino, possible Portrait of Alessandro Braccesi,
1480, Uffizi

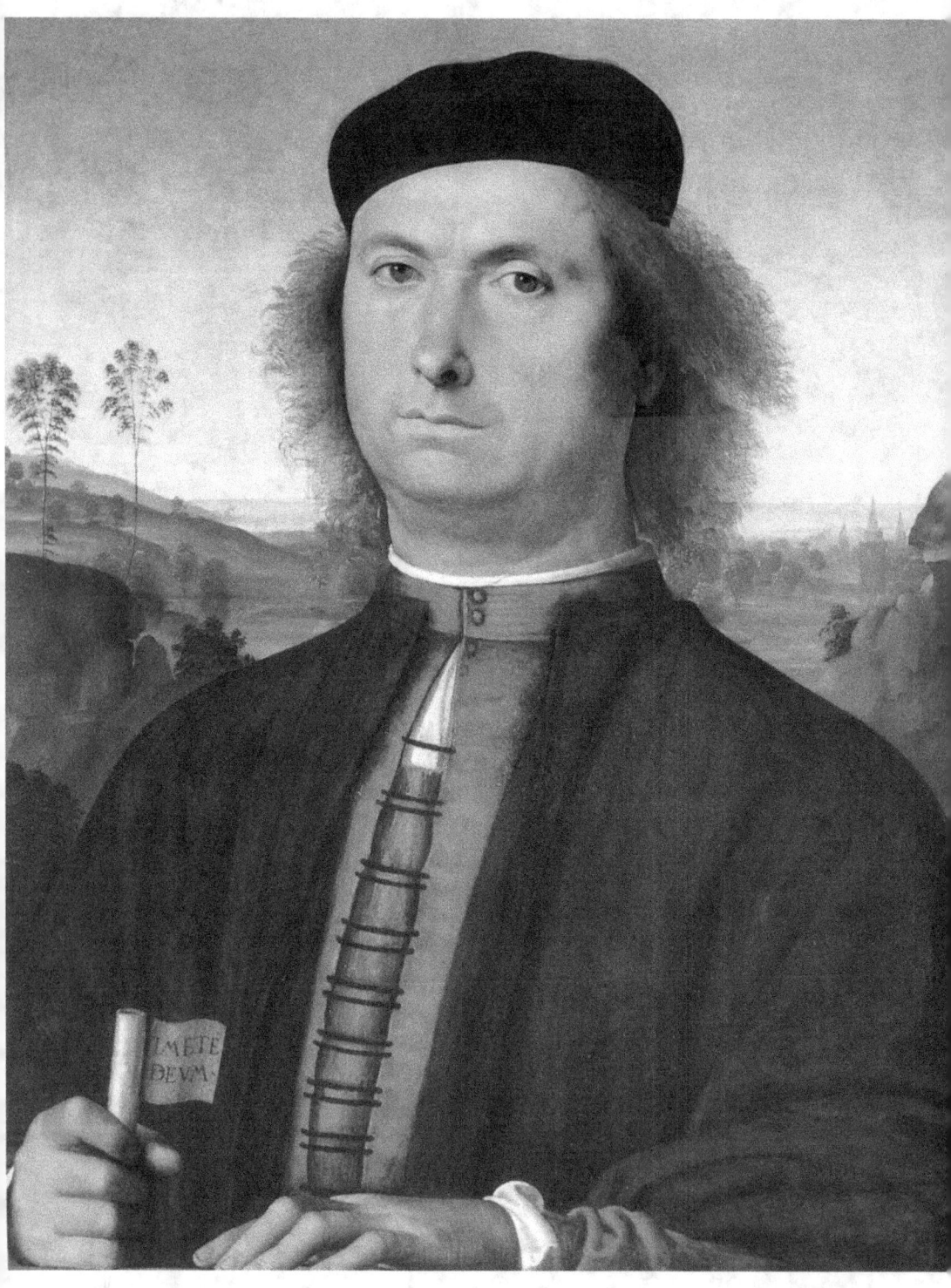

Perugino, Francesco delle Opere, 1494, Uffizi

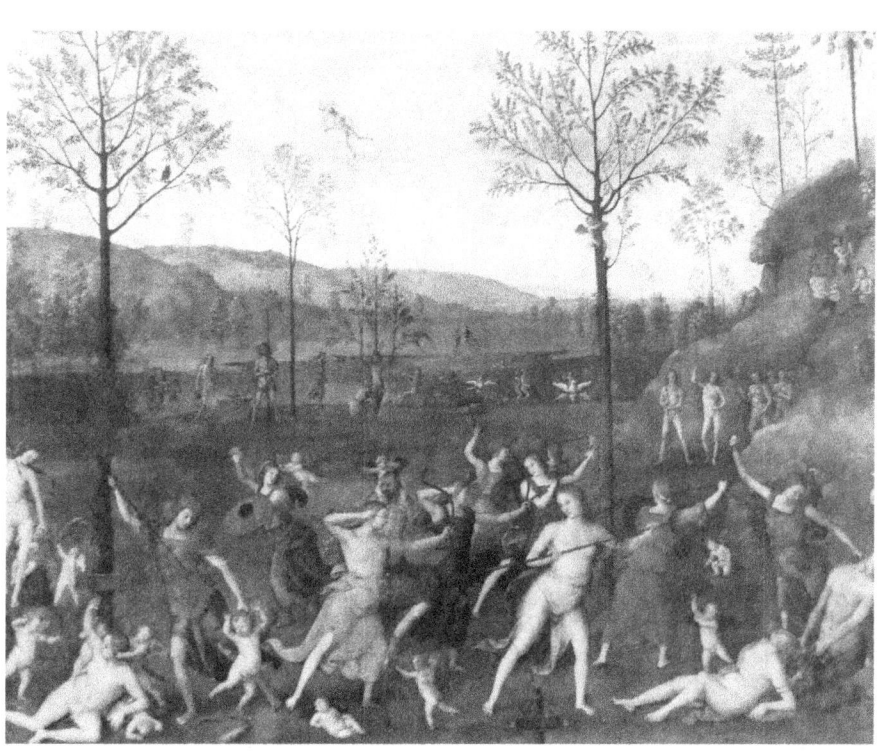

Perugino, The Battle of Love and Chastity, 1503-05

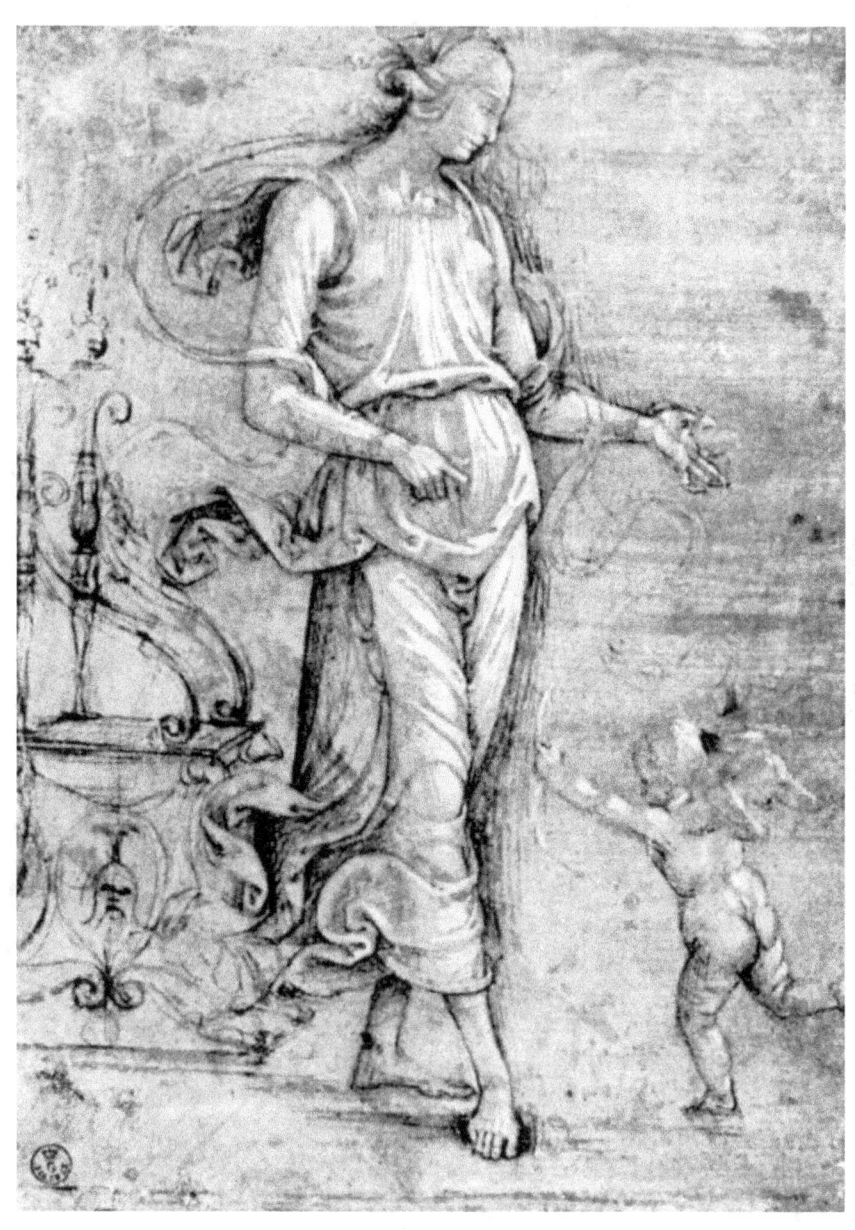

Perugino, Venus and Cupid, 1497-1500, Uffizi Gallery

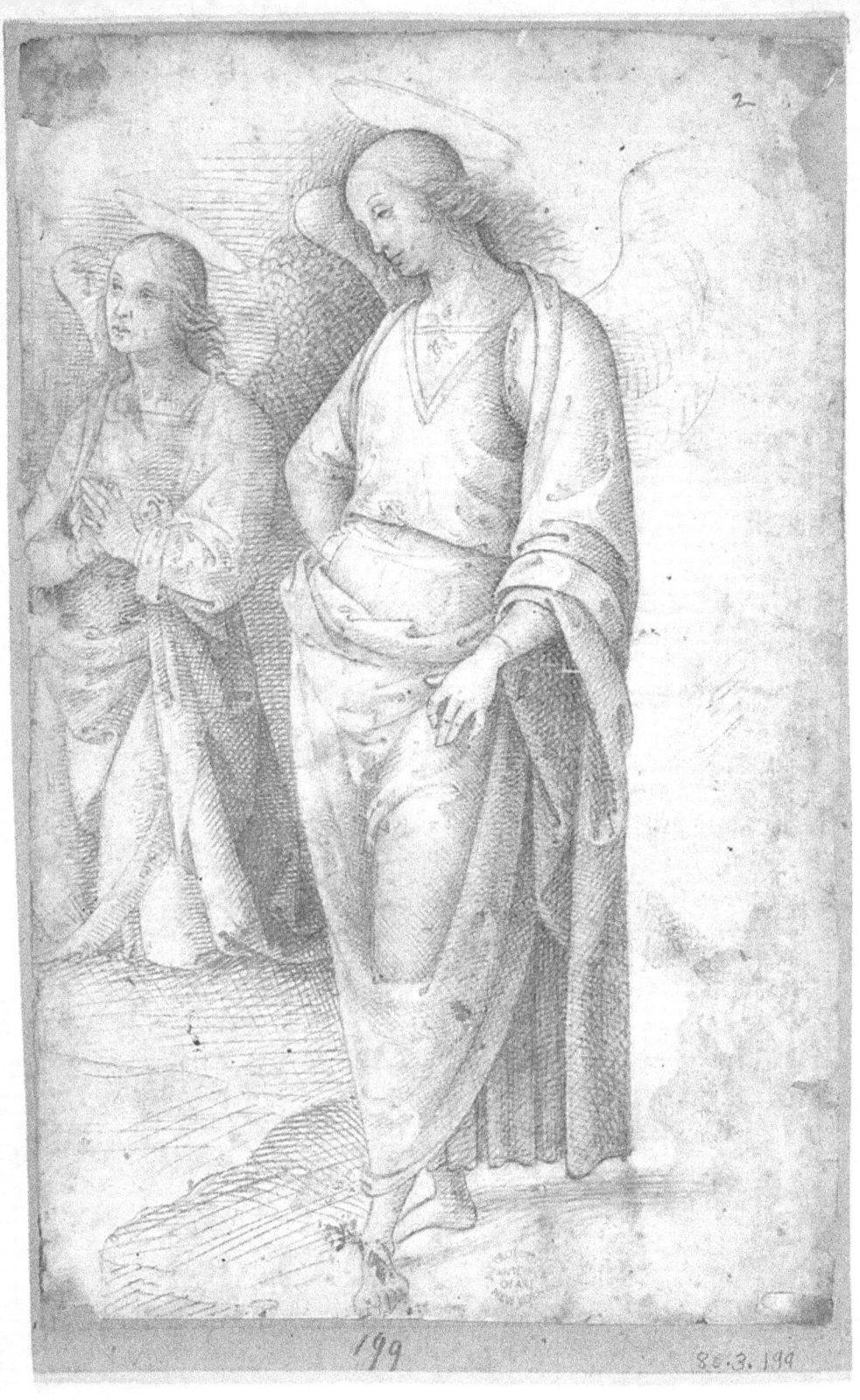

Perugino, Two Figures of Angels Standing,
Metropolitan Museum of Art, NYC

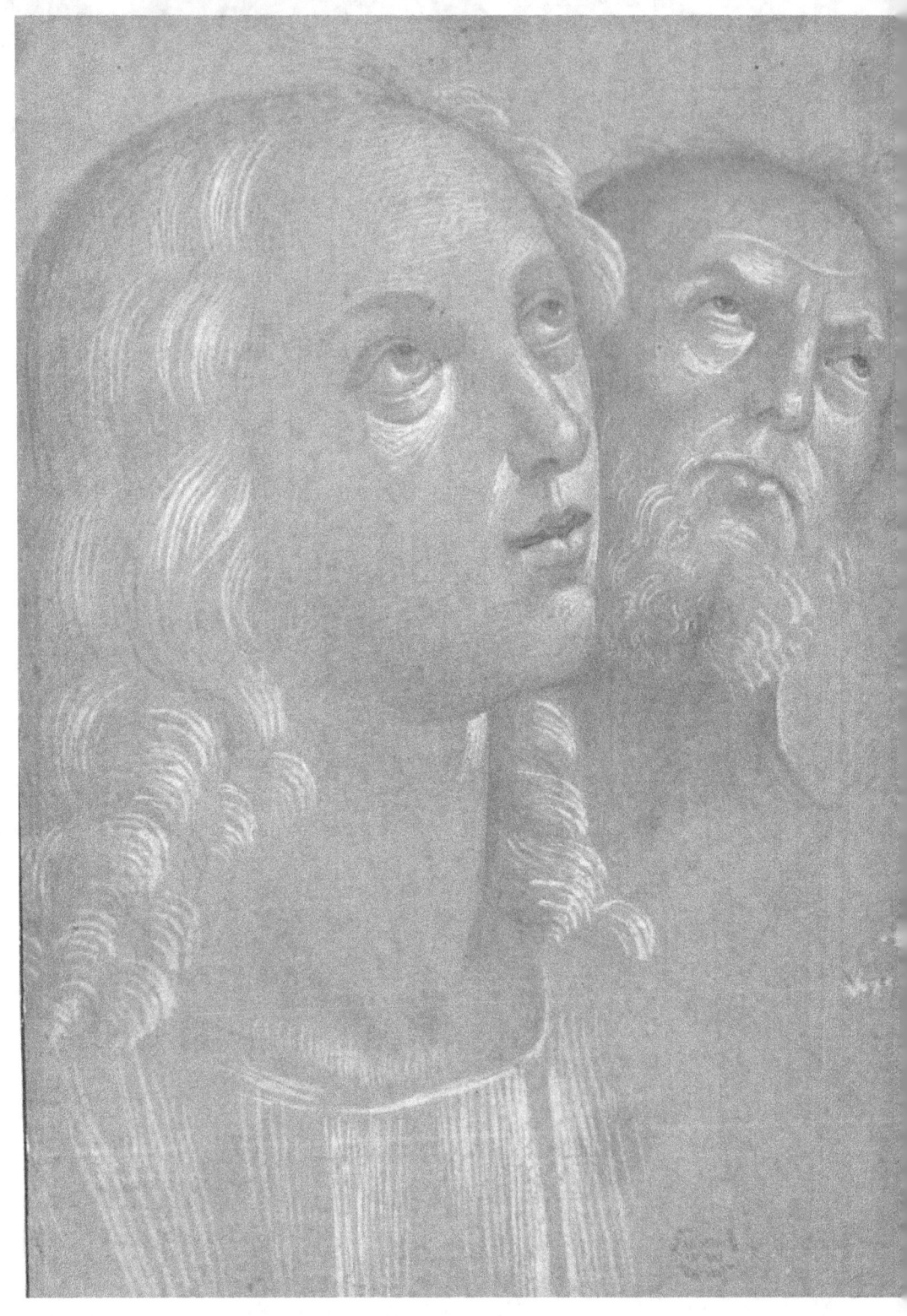

Perugino, Heads of Two Saints, Metropolitan Museum of Art, NYC

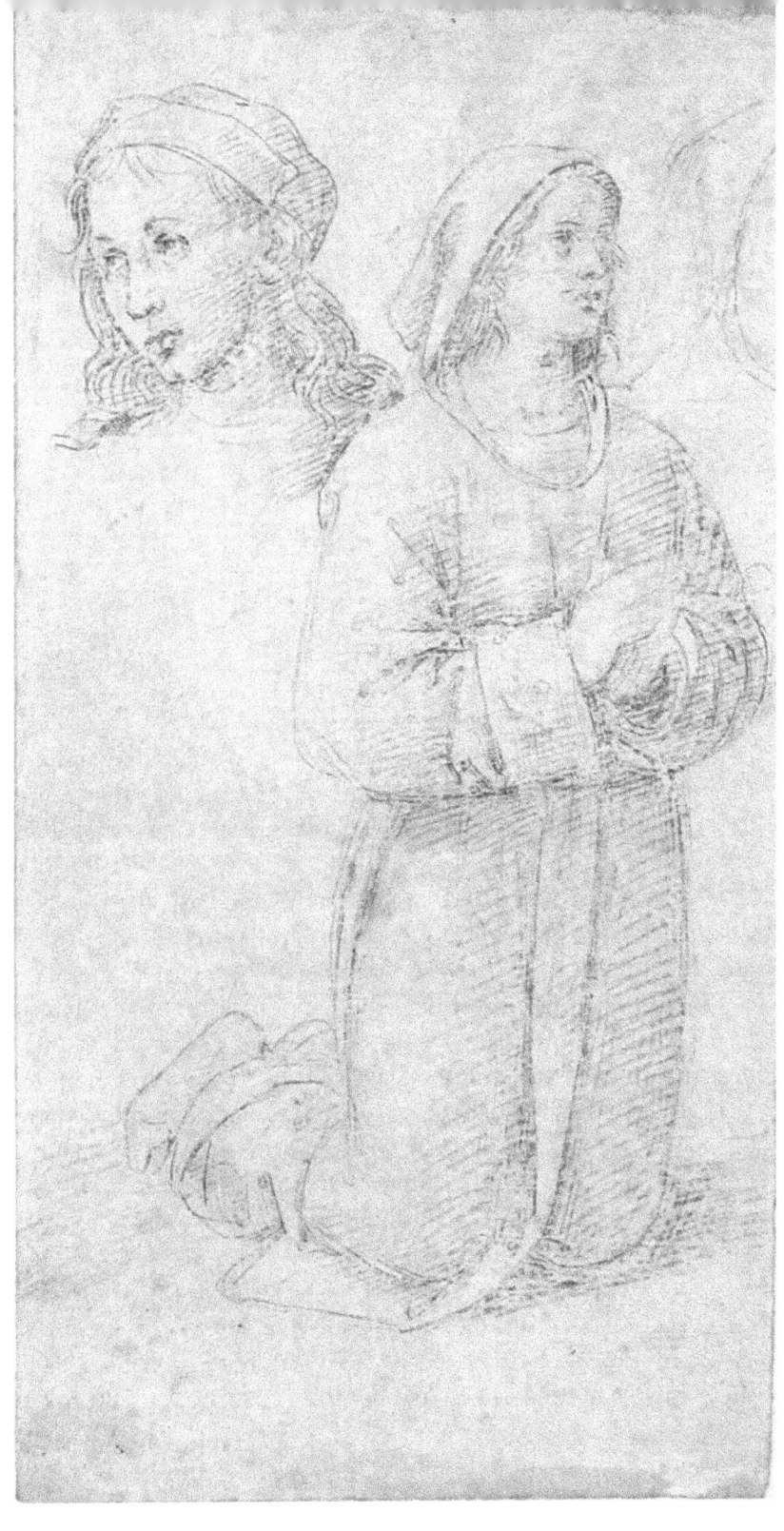

Perugino, Study of a Kneeling Youth,
and of the Head of Another, 1500, New York

CHAPTER VI

IN FULL STRENGTH

In the early spring of the year 1496 Perugino was in Venice, but in the autumn back in Florence and in Perugia, although possibly the winter saw him in Bologna. In 1497 he was in Florence, in Perugia, and in Fano. In 1498 he was in Florence, and then again at Fano.

The proof that Perugino was in Florence in 1496 consists in the document quoted by Morelli recording the purchase of certain land in Florence with a view to a permanent residence in the city.

To this year Morelli attributes the "Sposalizio" from the chapel of the Anello at Perugia, which is now at Caen. Vasari states that "for the altar of the Sacrament where the ring with which the Virgin Mary was espoused is preserved, this master painted an altar-piece representing the Marriage of Our Lady." Mariotti quotes Vasari, and on his evidence gives the picture to him, and every succeeding writer, including Crowe and Cavalcaselle, and Morelli, continues the ascription.

What is quite clear is that the company of St. Guiseppe received, as Mariotti records, the grant of a subsidy for an altar-piece; but Professor Adam Rossi states that up to November 1500 the picture had not been commenced. To 1500, therefore, Crowe attributes this picture, Morelli putting it earlier, in 1496. On these attributions a theory has been built up that Raphael in his "Sposalizio" (painted in 1503 or 1504) took as his *motif* the picture painted by his master Perugino, and improved considerably on the original conception. Crowe and Cavalcaselle in their inspection of the picture refer to its most striking quality, "its bright colouring," and qualify their praise by stating that "the tones have not the glow" of the master's usual work, and that "the forms are less pliant than of old." It is exactly these features that first attract the spectator and which, I must confess, puzzled me very considerably.

A little closer examination revealed the strange inequality in the surface of the picture, the stringiness and lumpiness of the draperies and the streaky character of the background. Much of my perplexity, however, ought not to have existed, inasmuch as in the *Gazette des Beaux Arts*, April 1896, Mr. Berenson had carefully examined the whole question, and ascribed the picture not to Perugino at all, nor to an earlier period than the Raphael "Sposalizio," but to the hand of Lo Spagna, and since 1504. With his opinion, although contrary to the accepted judgment, I am in the fullest accord, and I think that Vasari, going only upon hearsay, and with probably only a casual glance at the picture, if ever he saw it at all, makes a grave mistake when he attributes it to Pietro. Mr. Berenson examines all the evidence pro and con with his usual ability, and produces, in my opinion, over-whelming proof of his attribution. He compares the "Sposalizio" with the pictures by Lo Spagna in other places, the "Virgin and Child" at Perugia, the "Nativity" and the "Madonna and Child" at the Louvre, and the "Coronation of the Virgin," Lo Spagna's greatest work (dated 1511), and preserved at Todi.

He points out that several of the faces in these pictures are identical with faces at Caen, notably the face of the Virgin, which in every way, even in position, is the counterpart of the one in the "Nativity" in Paris. He finds the face of St. Joseph in more than one of Spagna's pictures, and especially he refers to a figure in the

Caen picture, the fourth to the right, a woman wearing a hood, which never once appears in any work of Perugino's, but which does appear, line for line, not only in the Todi "Coronation," but in another of Spagna's pictures. Other points of close resemblance are to be found in the drawing of the ears, which are totally different to those of Perugino's figures; in the hands, which are broad and heavy in the Caen picture and in Lo Spagna's usual work, but fine and delicate in Perugino's; and especially in the colouring, certain special tints such as a chartreuse-green and rose-salmon appearing in the Caen and Todi pictures, and never once to be found in Perugino's accepted work.

One very instructive set of arguments Mr. Berenson draws from a close examination of Raphael's "Sposalizio" at Milan. Its shape is upright. Perugino always represented the scene in a long, narrow panel, the position of the Virgin and St. Joseph, and of the branch carried by St. Joseph, are entirely antithetical to the Umbrian fashion, while, curiously enough, Lorenzo Costa, who was probably a fellow-pupil of Raphael's, under the influence of Timoteo Vite, painted in about 1504 or 1505 a "Sposalizio," upright as is this one, at Caen, and agreeing with it in many other ways. A masterly piece of reasoning shows that Raphael's work is of the Ferrarese school and not of the Umbrian, and that instead of its being a souvenir of the Caen picture, and based upon it and greatly improved, it is, in fact, an original work upon which Lo Spagna based his picture which is now at Caen. When to these arguments are added the want of style and dignity in the Bramantesque temple at Caen, the absence of the colonnade that Perugino favoured, and which he drew from Piero della Francesca, the want of intermediate grouping, the stubborn heaviness of the draperies, so different from Perugino's light, easy folds, the hard, empty density of the foliage, the change in the distant scenery, and the absence of horizon and cloud, and finally the entirely different drawing of the feet from the manner in which Perugino drew them, the case is practically proved, and to Lo Spagna must the Caen picture be attributed. If further evidence were needed, it is ready to hand in the fact that not one Perugian letter, document, or writer attributes the "Sposalizio" to Perugino, although all speak of it with great terms of reverence, while Vasari alone gives it to Vannucci, and, as is well known, his attributions must often be taken *cum grano salis.*

Having in all this agreed most gladly with Mr. Berenson, I must now part company with him in reference to another picture attributed to this same year.

Few pictures have exercised critics more than has the "Apollo and Marsyas" in the Louvre.

This charming little work was purchased by Mr. Morris Moore as a Mantegna. When sold to the Louvre in 1883 for 200,000 francs, it was agreed that it should be placed in the Salon Carré, under the title of "Raphael de Morris Moore."

It is still called a Raphael in the Louvre catalogue, although a note is added which only commits the authorities to the statement that it is unquestionably the work of an Umbrian artist. Morelli put it first to Timoteo Vite, but confesses that he did not examine it carefully. In a later work he withdrew this ascription, and says that "it belongs most probably to a master whose style is in close affinity with that of Perugino." Mr. Berenson includes it in his list of Perugino's works, but I am much more inclined to leave the attribution where Morelli left it.

The two figures are quite nude. This is almost a unique circumstance with Perugino, the only other nude figures in his pictures being some distant ones in his "Love and Chastity." Here is, therefore, a most exceptional circumstance; and also the absence of any drapery deprives the critic of one of the most definite marks, the dark hollows, by which Perugino's work is identified. Furthermore, there are birds in the sky, and I know of no sky of Perugino's in which they appear. The feet of the two figures are very Peruginesque, the open and upward curling great toe is clearly defined; but the hands have not the awkward tong shape of his earlier work, nor the very thin, boneless appearance of his mature work. The landscape and the trees are like those of Perugino; but the very prominent lyre has none of his characteristics, and in technique and handling is painted quite differently from Perugino's method. The picture seems much more likely to be the work of Pinturicchio, and, in any case, I cannot personally attribute it to Perugino.

I agree, however, with Mr. Claud Phillips in attributing the "St. Bernard" at Munich to this period of Perugino's life. It is, of course, impossible to fix its date exactly, but from 1496 to 1500 one may safely put it, and, as regards its serene beauty, hardly too much can be said. The picture was originally in the church of San Spirito in Florence, and there is now a copy of it in that place. King Ludwig I. bought it in 1829 from the Capponi family, who held the rights over the Nasi chapel, where it hung, and although it has been cleaned and restored, it remains a beautiful and quite genuine work. It is well to compare the hands and the ears in this picture, with their delicate, sensitive beauty, with the heavy features in the Caen picture, to which reference was lately made, and the comparison will be wholly satisfactory, and in every way in favour of Mr. Berenson's argument. An interesting study for this "Vision of St. Bernard" is at the Uffizi, and comparison may well be made with a picture by Lippo Lippi in the Badia, illustrating the same scene.

To this same period we attribute the "Virgin in Glory" at Bologna, the "Family of St. Anne" at Marseilles, and the master-piece in Florence, the "Crucifixion" of Sta. Maria Maddalena dei Pazzi. In the Bologna picture we see the lovely figure of St. Michael, to which allusion has already been made when reference was made to the Certosa altar-piece, now in the National Gallery. The great archangel is even fuller of beauty in this picture, his hands especially being of exquisite form and grace. There are three other adoring saints, St. Catherine of Alexandria, St. John the Divine, and St. Apollonia.

Above in the sky is the glowing mandorla of cherubs, a favourite device of Pietro's, glowing with rainbow radiance, and enveloping in its misty colour the cherub heads which belong to it. The conception is very lovely, the colouring subdued and sunny, and, while the picture recalls the Borgo and Lyons pictures, it yet foreshadows the great Vallombrosan "Assumption" which the master was to produce a few years later on.

The Marseilles picture is remarkable in many ways. It represents a scene that was very seldom selected by the old masters, and which no one treated so beautifully as did Perugino. There are, perhaps, not more than half-a-dozen examples amongst all the old masters' pictures which represent the "Family of St. Anne," and yet the subject is one that is particularly worthy of careful and thoughtful treatment. Perugino has adopted a very fine arrangement. The Virgin is enthroned in the centre, and has the divine Child on her knee. Behind her stands St. Anne in a very motherly attitude, resting her two hands on her daughter's shoulders. On the right of the throne stands St. Mary Salome, holding in her arms St. John the Divine, and by her side is St. Joachim, the husband of St. Anne. At their feet stands the child St. James. On the opposite side, to the left of the throne, stands St. Mary, the wife of Cleophas, holding in her arms St. James the Less. By her side stands St. Joseph, and near by another child, St. Joseph Justus. Two more children, St. Simon and St. Thaddeus, are seated on the steps of the throne, and above them is the inscription, PETRVS DE CHASTRO PLEBIS PINXIT.

The whole scene is under a wonderful and lofty archway, and beyond is an exquisite landscape of hills and rolling plain. The children are exquisite in grace and beauty, and two of them were copied by Raphael, and his picture still hangs in the sacristy of St. Pietro in Cassinense at Perugia. The artist has inscribed the name of each saint on the halo of light that surrounds each head, and the composition of the group is almost perfect, so well arranged and so well balanced. The colouring is subdued but radiant with sunlight, and few pictures are as typical of the master's hand. All his peculiarities of painting, his unusual draperies, his exaggerated feet, his long slender hands with lumpy knuckles, and his restful, quiet, self-contained figures can be studied in it.

Originally it was painted for the monastery of St. Anna, and later on was transferred to St. Maria de Fossi in Perugia, and was brought to Marseilles with the Perugian spoil which was mentioned in a preceding chapter. There is an early drawing for the whole picture at Alnwick.

The wonderful fresco at Sta. Maria Maddalena dei Pazzi was never seen by Crowe and Cavalcaselle or would have been recognised by them as one of the artist's grandest conceptions. In Crowe's time, the permission of the Archbishop of Florence was needed ere the picture could be inspected, and this permission Crowe could not obtain. The chapter-house in which it is situate is now secularised, and the fresco can be seen. Vasari speaks of the monastery under its old name of the Cestello, and records that a picture of St. Bernard was also painted for the same house, but this has been lost. The great fresco in question was ordered in 1493, for 55 ducats, by Pietro Pucci and his wife Giovanna, and was finished in this eventful year April 20th, 1496. The scene is represented under three arches. In the central one is the Crucifix, its arms stretching from wall to wall of the arch, its foot on the ground, and its upper extremity nearly touching the crown of the arch. At its foot kneels the Magdalen, gazing tenderly up at the crucified Christ, above the cross are the eclipsed sun and moon. On the left are the two figures of the Virgin and St. Bernard, and on the right are two more figures, St. John the Divine and St. Benedict.

There are only these six figures in the entire picture, which covers the whole wall of the chapter-house, but beyond them the arches seem to reveal a great Umbrian landscape, which stretches farther than eye can reach. It is practically the same view as can be seen from the city of Perugia, from the hill of Montefalco or from the monastery of Assisi, and is apparently limitless. There are the long sweeping outlines of the Umbrian Hills, the distant towns with their churches and castles, the pleasant waters winding in and out of the hills and gleaming in the evening light, and the delicate larch and olive trees crowning the hills and standing out so clearly and daintily against the sky, while above and filling nearly half of the archway space is the blue and purple sky, flecked with white gossamer clouds and reaching far up in its hollow dome beyond the range of sight.

As the spectator steps into the quaint chapter-house, this whole scene appears to open into view. The central crucifix with its solemn burden, and the five quiet figures standing so still and placid, full of that intense sorrow and tender pity which absorb the whole being, and which are so evidently the dominant passions that the mind of the spectator unites with them, and all who gaze on this sublime scene do so with reverend pity for the central figure, and intense sympathy for the spectators in the drama. There are two studies in existence for this work, one for the Christ on the Cross, on the back of a drawing of Pericles (252, 400) and the other for the standing figure of the Virgin (251, 417). Both are in the Uffizi Gallery. In the central compartment of the fresco will be recognised the prototype of the "Crucifixion" by Raphael now belonging to Mr. Ludwig Mond. There is, however, far more pure beauty, definite purpose, and tender reverence in the work by Perugino than in that by the youthful Raphael, although the merit of the latter work is very great, and surprisingly so when the age of the artist is taken into consideration. There is a breadth and power and an originality about Raphael's figure that is wonderful, but from the point of view of reverence and devotion, Perugino's marvellous and touching creation is superior to it.

The Certosa altar-piece, now in the National Gallery, is usually considered to be one of the greatest pictures Perugino ever executed. One-sixth part of it only is still *in situ*, the central panel of the upper tier. This represents the Eternal Father within a mandorla of cherubs. The remaining five panels are copies, the two upper ones, after Borgognone, to replace originals in France, the three lower ones to replace the originals in London.

There are one or two points that merit special attention in this picture. It is desirable to mention that what has been called the monotony of Perugino can be clearly seen at this time. The figure of St. Michael has already appeared in the Albani altar-piece, and will appear again in the Bologna "Assumption," and other pictures.

The elaborately decorated shield and the quaint head-dress of the great archangel appear in the figures of the Cambio decoration, in the "Sposalizio," and in the Sistine Chapel fresco. The angels which appear in the central panel will be marked again and again in later works.

Perugino in his lifetime was severely criticised for this failing. Lanzi expressly records the grumbling of many of Perugino's patrons at his want of variety in treatment, the fact that his altar-pieces more or less closely resembled one another, and the artist's reply that he robbed no one. His figures were admired in one picture, why should they not be in another? and if a figure was pronounced lovely and suitable at one time and for one place, why should it be condemned when used for a similar position in another place.

This complaint, made in the fifteenth century, has continued down to the present time, and has certain justification. There is a want of originality about Perugino's conceptions beyond a certain point; but this very monotony is a most useful aid in recognising and scheduling his pictures, while individually his figures are so graceful, and his groups so well composed, that those who love Umbrian art never tire of gazing upon his fascinating pictures.

This great altar-piece was completed in 1499. In the early part of that year the Duke of Milan, Il Moro, wrote to the monks at Pavia complaining of the delay in the completion of the altar-piece he had commissioned, speaking of the large sum he had disbursed, and of his love for the Certosa and desire to see it completed, and begging the Carthusians to hurry on Perugino to complete his work. They did so, and by the end of 1499 the picture was in its place.

In the following year, 1497, Perugino was in Fano, and there again in 1498. In each of these years he was probably also in

Perugia, and in one of them, perhaps 1497, he was at Sinigaglia and at Cantiano, two small places close to Fano. Of his visits to Fano we have two results: a "Madonna and Child with Saints," dated 1497, and an "Annunciation," dated 1498; while at Sinigaglia there is a "Madonna and Child with Saints" closely resembling the Fano one, and at Cantiano a "Holy Family" of similar characteristics. In the intervals which enabled the artist to revisit Perugia we have evidence of his work in a "Madonna and Child," dated 1497, now in the Gallery of Perugia, and in another picture attributed to the same period and now hanging in the same gallery. Even these visits do not complete his wanderings, for on the 26th of June 1498 he was certainly in Florence.

It is only an assumption on my part that the Sinigaglia and Cantiano pictures followed the Fano ones. They may have just preceded them, and should perhaps belong to that already crowded year 1496, but I am strongly of opinion that such is not the case. Again, they should perhaps be given to a later period altogether, say to 1500 or 1501; but we have no evidence whatever connecting Perugino with this remote part of the sea-coast save in 1497 and 1498, and as in style and colouring, even in composition and design, the Sinigaglia and Cantiano pictures so closely resemble those at Fano, and the places were not easy of access save from Fano, and we do not hear of the artist being in this district on any other occasion, the attribution to that period is given.

Both of these pictures have signs of hurried execution, and do not appear to be in all their details the work of the master, and my contention is that they were planned when the Fano ones were in progress and executed partly by pupils under the control of the artist who was himself working close at hand. The 1497 altar-piece at Fano is really a fine picture, and the five predella pictures are remarkably good, perhaps the finest of this style of miniature-like painting that Perugino ever executed. In the predella scene can be noted Perugino's method of representing the "Sposalizio," and the arcade and temple doorway, the arrangement and grouping of the figures, and the open air effect of the whole, and entire absence of crowding will all be noted as characteristics which the Caen picture does not possess. The lunette of this fine altar-piece is the same scene as the artist used in the scattered altar-piece for St. Agostino, and should be compared with the lunette from this altar-piece which now hangs in St. Pietro in Cassinense at Perugia. In the latter the Virgin and the Magdalen are each holding one of the hands of the dead Christ. In the Fano picture these hands hang down loosely and rest on the tomb. In other respects the two pictures are almost identical.

The other Fano picture is a very charming "Annunciation." The arched colonnade again appears. The Eternal Father, within a circular mandorla, is above, and below, flying towards the Madonna, is the white dove of the Holy Spirit. In the distance is Fano itself, and in the far distance the sea.

We now come to the two Perugia pictures. The one which is known to have been painted in 1497 for the altar of the noble confraternity of "San Pietro Martire," represents the Madonna seated upon a throne or tomb, crowned, and holding the Christ on her knee. Above in the air are two angels kneeling in adoration, while on the ground around and partially behind the Queen of Heaven, are two groups of white-robed penitents. There is a study for this picture in the Uffizi.

It ought to be quite easy to discover the exact date of the other picture. It was painted for the noble confraternity "della Giustizia," who deposited it in the gallery, and it evidently alludes to the union of the original confraternity of San Andrea della Giustizia, with a smaller but similar body dedicated to San Bernardino and connected with the church of San Francesco. San Bernandino of Siena is one of the two saints who are kneeling in the foreground, and is distinguished by the tablet bearing the I.H.S. surrounded by rays of light which floats in the air close to him. He lived at the convent of San Francesco al Prato, and close to the convent now stands the oratory dedicated in 1461 to his memory, the front of which is decorated with Agostino Ducci's wonderful marble and terra-cotta façade. The confraternity for whom the picture was painted, specially honoured the memory of San Bernardino, and therefore had a peculiar devotion toward his patron saint, St. Francis of Assisi. St. Francis, in the picture in question, kneels opposite to San Bernardino. In the background is a large group of kneeling people headed by the Priori in their furred gowns, and near at hand are women and penitents, all intent upon the same petition. Still more remote is a representation of the city, differing in many respects from the view of Perugia given in the St. Agostino altar-piece painted in 1521, and resembling much more closely the town of San Gemignano as it now appears.

One would have naturally expected that this picture would have been named by Mariotti, or that documents in Orsini or in the Perugian archives would have mentioned it. My chief reason for giving it to 1498 is that in that year there was an outbreak of plague in the city which the records inform us suddenly ceased in response to great supplication, and it is possible that this picture was painted for the confraternity in commemoration of this answer to prayer. There are perhaps only two other instances in which St. Francis is represented, but the reason already stated may well account for his presence in this picture.

The "Crucifixion," now in the Accademia, may, I think, be ascribed to this period. It is an altar picture, and was painted for the Convent of St. Jerome in Florence, and there is definite evidence that in 1498 Perugino did visit Florence and painted a picture in the city. There is much in this work which recalls the Pazzi "Crucifixion." The Christ is from the same model, but is a larger figure in every way and not quite so carefully drawn as in the Pazzi one. Its increased size and more hurried execution gives it a coarser and harsher effect. The Pazzi "Crucifixion" has but one figure at the foot of the cross. The Accademia necessarily has two, as St. Jerome, with his lion and hat, had to be introduced. The Blessed Virgin is the same figure as in the Pazzi fresco, and in the same posture even to the twisting of the fingers in the clasped hands, but her feet are bare in the Pazzi fresco and in the St. Jerome picture are adorned with elaborate sandals.

The scene at the back of the cross in the Pazzi fresco is evidently not Florence, and was probably either a typical Umbrian town or one connected in some way with the donor's early life; but in the St. Jerome picture the city that is depicted is clearly Florence, and certain towers and spires can be recognised in the scene. The composition is more crowded than in the Pazzi fresco, and this element and the heavier treatment of the crucified Figure somewhat detract from its beauty; but it is probable that the explanation of the whole circumstance is that the St. Jerome "Crucifixion" was intended to be placed high up above an altar and at the end of a long and somewhat dark church, whereas the Pazzi "Crucifixion" was on a level with the eye, rising up from the ground, and in a small and well-lighted chapter-house.

CHAPTER VII

THE CAMBIO

It has already been shown that the statement of Crowe and Cavalcaselle that Pietro resided entirely in Florence at this time is incorrect, but it is quite open to believe that he had desired to do so. He invested some of his earnings in the purchase of land in the Borgo Pinti in 1498, and in the deed is referred to as "habitator in populo S. Petri Majoris." In January 19th, 1497, he was called in to assist Benozzo Gozzoli, Cosimo Roselli, and Filippino Lippi to value the frescoes of Alesso Baldovinetti in the church of Sta. Trinità in Florence, and in June 1498 he was present at a meeting called to discuss the repairs of the lantern of Sta. Maria del Fiore.

The church had been struck by lightning, and the question of the repair of the injured lantern was submitted to a meeting of architects, sculptors, and painters, and at this meeting Filippino Lippi, Lorenzo di Credi, and Perugino all tendered their advice. At about this time came an invitation from the Priori of Perugia for him to undertake the entire decoration of their Cambio or Bourse; and this invitation seems to have finally disposed of the Orvieto contract. He wrote to the Orvietans stating that he could not come as he was otherwise engaged; and there is no trace of his ever visiting their city during his life.

The flattering request of his adopted townsmen was well pleasing to Perugino; the terms offered him were satisfactory; and early in 1499 he left Florence and commenced in Perugia what I consider to be the most important work of his life.

The scenes in the decoration of what is still called in Perugia the "Noble Cambio," are not the most beautiful that Pietro painted, nor are they the finest of his works in the way of drawing, composition, or colouring. They, however, form part of a complete scheme of decoration, carried out, it is true, under certain definite restrictions laid down by the Priori, but, subject to these restrictions, designed throughout by the master, and mainly executed by his own hand.

It has already been said that to understand Perugino it is absolutely necessary to visit Umbria. The dictum can be made even more definite. It is needful to see not only Umbria but Perugia, and not only Perugia but the Cambio, in order to have an adequate idea of the artist's power. The quaint little room must be visited again and again if the student is to really understand its beauty. When at first one steps from the brilliant sunshine of the street into this dark chamber, it is not easy to realise the rich decoration which covers its walls. Gradually, however, as the eye becomes accustomed to the more subdued light, it reveals itself, but part only of the room can be studied at a time. The room is very much as Pietro left it, and in its way is one of the most beautiful in all Italy.

The lower part of the walls is wainscotted with dark wood inlaid in tarsiature. Near the entrance is the throne for the judge, and below it the desks and seats for the money-changers, all exquisitely carved, and then all around the room, above the wainscotting, is Perugino's fresco decoration, and above it the vaulted ceiling painted from his designs by his pupils. There is unity about the whole which is perfect. Perugino is at his best, straining his utmost to give honour to the town of his adoption, stimulated by the very nature of his commission, exercising all the fertility of his talent in design, and labouring with intense sympathy and determination, convinced that in Perugia he can execute a work that will perpetuate his name for ever and ever.

The decoration is curiously illustrative of that strange mingling of spirits which the Renaissance produced. The popular mind at this period was deeply affected by the study of the classics, and sacred and profane literature were being considered side by side. The predominant spirit was certainly Christian and not pagan, but in a building intended for secular work the classic spirit had a fuller development than in a church, and, as Perugino frankly stated in the contract for the decoration that his aim was "to recommend the merchants and magistrates therein assembled never to forsake the path of duty, but to remain faithful to the dictates of wisdom, of natural reason, and of religion," so it was quite admissible for him to appeal to great classic heroes for the lessons he desired to teach, and to emphasise and spiritualise all by the teaching of pure and humble Christianity.

It appears from Mariotti and Marchesi that the subjects were submitted to Pietro on the part of the Priori by Francesco Maturanzio, Professor of Rhetoric at Perugia, and secretary to the Priori. In a MS. of poetical works by Maturanzio, still preserved at Perugia, the inscriptions on the tablets of the decoration appear, and Maturanzio himself, according to Marchesi, derived some of his inspiration from a MS. Cicero, in which are miniatures of the Virtues and of the classic heroes who specially exemplify them. Near the door Pietro has painted Cato, then on the left wall, in two bays, are groups of philosophers and warriors in groups of three, each group consisting of a Greek between two Romans, and underneath each figure is his name. Above are representations of the Virtues, and opposite to these two bays is one in which are depicted the "Prophets and Sibyls," while at the end of the room appear the "Nativity" and the "Transfiguration."

These figures are arranged in one long line, each figure standing separately apart from the others, lonely and abstracted. The warriors are singularly unlike what a more pagan artist would have depicted. They are dainty, dreamy, gentle knights, almost feminine in their grace of limb and countenance, and in their elegance of costume and pose. In their head-dresses the fancy of the artist has run wild. Nothing is too extraordinary for Perugino to devise, and, fond as he always was of eccentric helmets and mitres, he has given full play to his imagination in these Cambio groups, and decked his heroes in the most extraordinary and extravagant helmets that even his fancy could invent. The armour and the costume of the figures also show how exuberant was the artist's fancy, and in the shape and decoration of the shields especially he gave it full play. Despite all these drawbacks, there is a certain stately grace about the figures, the drawing is accurate, the proportions good, and the attitudes natural, although just a little forced. The most important work of all is in the large bay opposite to the warriors and philosophers. This is styled the "Triumph of Religion," and represents the Prophets and the Sibyls standing together in converse, and above them is the Eternal Father, who is attended by two angels, and who is raising His hand in blessing. There is more power, breadth, and movement in this group than in the others, and there is closer connection between the various figures. They are more certainly interested one in the other, and in conversation one with the other; while as regards their draperies there is a broad, full sweeping treatment that is very marked, and deserves careful attention.

One more point may well be noted, that, fond as Perugino was of inscriptions and names on his pictures, of Latin verses, and of Latin signatures, in none of them is there such a profusion of inscriptions as in the Cambio, and every letter is most carefully drawn with the pencil, and is admirable in its proportions and clearness. One scene is practically unique. On but one other occasion, as far as I am aware, did Perugino paint the "Transfiguration," and then he carried out but little of the picture himself. Vasari incorrectly styles it the "Resurrection." This latter scene Pietro represented many times, and even Crowe and

Cavalcaselle, careful as they usually were, have confused the "Transfiguration" with the "Resurrection" when they refer to the Fano altar-piece. The three disciples in the Cambio fresco are grouped very much in the way in which Pietro grouped the sleeping disciples in the Accademia picture. The attitude of the Christ closely resembles that of the Christ in the Vatican "Resurrection"; but, this resemblance accepted, the connection between the two representations is at an end.

There are no angels in this picture, which, for Perugino, is most unusual; but Moses and Elias, fine, well-drawn, powerful figures, take the place of the usual singing angels who float in the sky. The half-startled look of the disciples is very cleverly presented, and the glow of the ethereal light upon their faces, partially warded off by St. John with his upraised hand, is beautifully depicted.

The transfigured Christ is an imposing figure, full of dignity and peace, and demanding reverence from those around. There is a sense of space, of distance, and of mystery in this fine fresco, which Perugino seldom, if ever, exceeded.

When, at the very close of his life, Perugino painted for Sta. Maria Nuova his other fresco of the "Transfiguration," he used the same cartoon as he adopted for the Cambio, reversing the three figures on the ground. The result is, however, far different, and but little of the fresco is really the work of Perugino. In place of a mandorla of rays of burning light, there is the usual one of cherubs, cut across by an awkward cloud, and almost all the figures have lost their dignity and power.

His fellow-citizens paid him the compliment of desiring that his portrait should be identified with his important work, and probably Maturanzio composed the complimentary verses which are written beneath it, and which Perugino himself could certainly not have selected. The inscription runs:

Perdita si fuerat pingendi his retulit artem;
Si nunquam inventa est hactenus ipse dedit,

which Rev. H. R. Ware has thus rendered:

If we had lost the painter's art, 'tis here restored in better part;
If it had always been unknown, he's given it as his very own.

The portrait of the artist may well be compared with the one in the Uffizi, which was so long believed to be his, but which has now been removed from its old position and hung in the Tribuna as the portrait of Francesco delle Opere, according to the inscription on its back.

With the knowledge that the one in the Cambio is genuine, it is surprising that the Uffizi portrait should for so long have been called Perugino's, and a whole story spun to account for the words "Timete Deum" which occur in the man's hand.

In not one feature do the two portraits, however, resemble one another, and the one of Perugino in the Cambio reveals him as a man of strong, healthy appearance, of unusual determination and great power. The features reveal strong sense of ideality, good knowledge of form and of colour, and some dry, lurking humour of a cynical and malicious type. To a certain extent the face is sensual, but not lascivious or voluptuous; but its main characteristic is its determination, the ability to conquer difficulties, to labour hard and long, and to produce a vast amount of work in a short time. It is also the face of a thoughtful man, not so much of a loveable one, as of one who was masterful and resolute.

Opposite to the portrait of the artist, close by the fresco of "Prophets and Sibyls," is a label with the words, "Anno Salvt M.D.," giving the definite information in what year the work was completed. It was, I take it, at this period of Perugino's life that the great Raphael first became his pupil. Vasari's statement as to Giovanni Santi taking the lad to Pietro is unconfirmed, and must be received with caution, especially as we know that Santi died in 1494.

As has already been shown, Perugino was wandering, in the years previous to 1500, far and wide, and was seldom at Perugia for long together; and, as Morelli was the first to point out, it would have been impossible for him to give the regular and continuous instruction to the young lad Raphael at that time. In 1504 Raphael painted his "Sposalizio," in 1505 the fresco at S. Severo in Perugia, and probably it was several years previous to this that he painted the Dudley "Crucifixion." Professor Rossi of Perugia has announced that documents exist in that city proving that Raphael actually did not leave Urbino till the end of 1499. The information is quite credible, and is what might be expected; but it lacks confirmation, and when at Perugia I was quite unable to verify its statement.

The question is still an open one. Morelli gives Raphael's earlier training to Timoteo Vite, but, to my mind, produces no distinct proof of the influence of Timoteo upon the young Raphael. It is perfectly certain that the lad was a pupil to Perugino, and it is, of course, possible – although hardly conceivable – that his tuition was taking place during the busy wandering years which preceded 1500. My own notion is that the tuition began in 1499 or 1500, and that Raphael, together with the other pupils, took his part in the Cambio decoration, probably in the work of the ceiling. There is, of course, a local tradition that in two of the faces in the fresco of "Prophets and Sibyls" are immortalised the features of Raphael and Pinturicchio. Nothing is more likely. Both pupils were of unusual and remarkable appearance, and the master may quite as well have used them as his models while working with them in the room. There can be no definite proof of what part Raphael took in the scheme of decoration, but it is pleasant to conceive him as working side by side with the master whose art influenced him so strongly, and between this time and that of 1505, when the San Severo fresco was executed, Raphael may well have been assisting Perugino in all his work, and learning from him the art in which in later days he was to reign so triumphantly as king.

For the Cambio decoration Perugino appears to have received 350 *large* gold ducats, but the final payment of the money is not

made till 1507, when the juror of the Cambio, Alberto de
Mansueti, records with pride the fact that he had finally settled
the Cambio payments and obtained Perugino's receipt in full,
dated 15th January 1507.

CHAPTER VIII

FLORENCE, PERUGIA, AND CITTA DELLA PIEVE

The date 1500 is attached to the great Vallombrosan altar-piece, and it must, therefore, have been executed immediately after the completion of the Cambio. Whether it was painted in Vallombrosa itself or not cannot be stated with accuracy; but the general impression given by the documents relating to the picture is that it was executed within the precincts of the religious house. Vasari states clearly that the picture was done *at* Vallombrosa, but his statements of this sort have always to be accepted with caution. It is, however, in this case more than probable that he is correct.

The picture, now in the Accademia, is one of the finest that Perugino ever produced. It presents, of course, many of Perugino's favourite figures and arrangements. The mandorla recalls the altar-pieces of Borgo and of Lyons. The Eternal Father above is similar to the scene in the "Prophets and Sibyls" fresco in the Cambio. The angels with musical instruments will be found again in the SS. Annunziata picture, and the archangels attending upon the Eternal Father have already been seen several times in earlier works. The general scheme of the picture is the one which Pietro made somewhat hackneyed, but there are certain special features that must not be overlooked. The Virgin is seated in the skies within a glowing radiance of pure white light, and this of itself is an unusual feature. Never has Perugino painted the Madonna so finely. There is a celestial beauty upon her face, and her hands and robe are depicted with the utmost skill and care. The angels are somewhat loosely drawn, insipid in countenance, and lacking in proportion, especially in their attenuated legs, and in the large size of their hands; but the artist's main attention has been given to three points in the picture – the figure of the Virgin, the four figures on the ground, and the landscape in the rear. Crowe and Cavalcaselle speak of the four attendant saints as "magnificent as isolated creations," and the words are none too strong.

The four figures are superb; they are well-balanced and stand firmly on their feet; their draperies are in easy folds, and are painted with unusual care, especially in their delicate gradations of colour; the pose is in each instance suitable and sufficient, and there is tender, reverent beauty in the faces, and the utmost dexterity and feeling in the painting of the hands.

Still greater work, however, Perugino executed at Vallombrosa. He painted the portraits of the Abbot Baldassare, and of Don Biagio Milanesi, and triumphantly proved his right to be termed a great portrait-painter. If all other works of Perugino had perished and we possessed these two heads alone, the genius of the artist would be revealed by them as of the highest order.

They are painted with the lightest of touch and with extra-ordinarily little colour. The tone is that of old yellow parchment, and each picture contains only the upturned head and a few inches of the brown monastic robe; but the effect is perfect. The marvellous feature, however, of each portrait is its absolute truth and its perfection of modelling. There is no accessory; there is no cap, or hood, or costume; there is only a plain brown background: but the effect is that of living, breathing life. The very slightest touches reveal the bones of the face and the corresponding hollows of the tightly-drawn skin. The bare, shaven head, with its narrow tonsure, allowed no opportunity for careless drawing. There was no hair with its rich shimmering colour to hide inaccuracies of line or to cover up faults in execution; but the master needed none of these excuses. The task was a stern one, uncompromising in its severity; but it is nobly executed, and two delineations of character are presented. Already allusion has been made to the portraits of Francesco delle Opere and of the artist himself, and if to them be added these two, and the faces of the standing figures in the Vallombrosan altar-piece, a careful student can hardly fail to acknowledge that the artist was, above all, a portrait-painter in the truest sense of the term.

There is a very puzzling picture which was probably painted at about this time, and which was executed for San Francesco in Perugia and hangs now in the Vatican Gallery. Vasari ascribes it to Perugino. Orsini suggests that Raphael had a hand in it. Crowe gives it entirely to Raphael as a very early work, and Morelli ascribes it entirely to the hand of Lo Spagna. In the midst of so many conflicting theories it may be allowable for me to agree with Vasari. It is not very likely that in all his work Perugino would preserve the same level of beauty. The master had, as was most natural, his successes and his failures. At times his commissions were so numerous that some of them were carelessly executed; at another time a subject was given him which did not altogether appeal to his mind; at another he worked *con amore*, and put his whole soul into his labour. We see fine results in the Cambio, and in the Vallombrosan pictures, and I take it these are followed by this "Resurrection," which is weak and unsatisfactory, and by others which are even at a lower level. Later on we shall see important work at Rome, in the Louvre, and at Città, followed by poor, inadequate work at Spello. Then comes a recrudescence, of which the great altar-piece at St. Agostino is the result, and this is followed by final work which is weak and monotonous, but which still retains the perfume of the master's nobler days.

The figure of the Saviour is inaccurate and badly drawn, the face is quite unsatisfactory, the mandorla clumsy and rigid, the angels poor and lacking in expression, and their draperies feeble. The colouring of the picture, the landscape, the faces and hands, the wonderful detail, the composition, the balance, and, above all, the technique, speak to me strongly of the master, to whom I ascribe the picture unhesitatingly. I can see no hand of Raphael in it, and while I see no special reason for our crediting the story that gives the sleeping soldier on the right the face of Raphael, yet even that statement but renders it less likely that Raphael had a hand in the picture itself, while I believe that a close comparison of the Cambio portrait with that of the flying soldier on the left will dispose of the theory that in his face we have delineated the countenance of the master himself.

We must now retrace our steps and look at the artist at Perugia. Mariotti records that in 1501 Perugino was one of the Priori of the City, and, being salaried officers, the Priori were obliged, according to Marchesi, to reside in the Palazzo Communale, and give daily attendance for magisterial business. This involved a good deal of civic duty, and doubtless consumed a great deal of time, and probably during 1501 Perugino did little painting. He was concerned also in domestic matters, as Orsini states that in two deeds, dated December 11th, 1501, and February 24th, 1502, he divided up certain property that had belonged to his uncle, Giovanni, and which devolved to himself and his two nephews, Agnolo and Giacomo di Giovanni. However, if he was at the moment unable to paint, he was prepared to make contracts for future work, and Mariotti records several of his interesting engagements.

One dated September 10th, 1502, is for some saints and angels around a large crucifix carved in wood, belonging to the convent of San Francesco al Monte, and for a "Coronation of the Virgin" to form the reverse side of this altar-piece. For that he was to have 120 florins. In the same year he agreed to supply to Baccio d' Agnolo designs for the intarsia work in the stalls of St. Agostino, which Baccio was to make in one year for 1120 florins, and for the due performance of his task Perugino became surety. He was also to paint a double altar-piece for St. Agostino, and was to design a frame for it which Tomaso was to carry out.

By another contract he agreed to paint a "Sposalizio" for the Duomo. This latter part of the contract I do not believe he ever carried out, and the St. Agostino altar-piece was not finished for nearly twenty years, as there is a record of its completion in a letter dated September 1521, written to the Podesta of Trevi, advising him that the Prior of St. Agostino had appointed a valuer for the picture, and begging him to apprise Perugino, who was then at Trevi, of the fact.

Other commissions recorded by Mariotti were the decorating of the doors of the palace, and the painting up of the arms of Pope Julius II., who three years after was to visit Perugia in state, and also the designing of a silver ship or *nef*, to be used as a credence table. Of all these various works he certainly executed at this time the double altar-piece for the Minorites at San Francesco al Monte, which has been removed to the Pinacoteca. Probably little more than the design for one side of this altar-piece was the work of Pietro, the execution being done by his pupils. The picture is in very bad condition, and in places seriously damaged, but there are certain features about it that distinguish it from Perugino's own work. The long chain of flowers and pearls carried by the angels is not Peruginesque. The master would have used a ribbon. The cloud which cuts across the mandorla in two places, the awkward, sentimental-looking faces of the disciples and women, the ill-drawn feet, and weak draperies, all reveal the hands of a pupil, yet the idea of the picture is distinctly Perugino's, and here and there are traces of firmer, stronger work, which may well be due to the master himself. The reverse side of the picture may, however, be safely ascribed to Perugino. The Virgin is the same as in the Pazzi "Crucifixion," while the figures of St. Mary Magdalen, St. Francis, and St. John, are to be found in other altar-pieces by Pietro in the same gallery. In its original condition the picture must have been a really fine one, and although terribly damaged, enough remains to show how tender and sympathetic must the whole composition have appeared. There is a rough grandeur about the quatrocento carved wood crucifix which is laid on the canvas; and the four figures and two angels grouped about it, so placid, and calm, and so full of simple sorrow, must have formed a very impressive work. The landscape is delicate and sunny, and there is every reason to consider this picture entirely the work of the master, and to regret very much that by reason of exposure, damp, and neglect it has so seriously suffered.

In 1503, Perugino left Perugia, so Mariotti records, completing in the October of that year the arms of Julius II. on the gates of the palace and on the five entrances to the city. He settled down in Florence in the Pinti quarter, and early in the year, on January 25th, 1504, was present at the meeting called to choose a place for Michel Angelo's gigantic statue of "David." This meeting resulted in some bitter controversy. There were eighteen artists present, amongst whom were Andrea della Robbia, Lorenzo di Credi, Sandro Botticelli, Perugino, Leonardo da Vinci, Filippino Lippi, David Ghirlandajo. Various positions were suggested for the statue, and a place under the Loggia met with the greatest approval. Lippi and the goldsmith Salvestro di Lavacchio having suggested that Michel Angelo himself would probably have given grave consideration to a site, Piero di Cosimo proposed that he should be given his choice. He chose the place occupied by the "Judith," which was removed, and the "David" taken to the Palazzo Vecchio. With this selection and decision Perugino did not agree, nor did those who voted with him for the position in the Loggia, and a party came into existence opposed to Michel Angelo and disliking his style. Many of these objectors were in the habit of meeting in the botega of Perugino's old friend, Baccio, the worker in intarsia, and on one of these occasions, when some remarks antagonistic to Michel Angelo were passed round, the sculptor, roused to exasperation, turned to Perugino and pronounced his paintings to be "absurd and antiquated." In the light of the new classic influence the statement was doubtless true, but it grievously annoyed Perugino, and he was foolish enough to appeal to the Council of Eight, but obtained no redress and only exposed himself to ridicule and sarcastic remarks.

Within a few days after these occurrences Perugino left Florence again, and went to Perugia. Here a letter reached him from the Priori of his birthplace, Città della Pieve, begging him to come and paint a fresco for them. On February 20th, 1504, he replied, stating that a fresco such as they required would cost two hundred florins, but that, in consideration of the commission being from his native town, he would reduce his charge to one hundred florins, twenty-five to be paid at once, and twenty-five every year for three years, and that he was prepared to start at the work as soon as he heard from the Priori. The price, even so reduced, was more than the Guild could afford, and further correspondence ensued. Eventually, Perugino wrote again, on March 1st, 1504, agreeing to abate another twenty-five florins and execute the work for seventy-five, and this the town of Città accepted. The two letters to which reference is made were discovered by Signor Guiseppe Bolleti of Città, in 1835. He was excavating a terrace of earth that made the wall damp on which is the famous fresco, and found in this earth a number of paint pots, and a tin tube of about 4 inches long containing these two letters, and a third one. Two are still preserved between sheets of glass at Città, and the third is in the gallery at Perugia, and my friend, Signor Andrea Ceccheti of Città della Pieve, has, by permission of the authorities of Città and of Perugia, photographed the three letters, so that I am able to present them in this book. Two are reproduced for the first time, the third was in Mezzanotte's scarce volume. The fresco covers a wall space of about 22 feet square. It is dated 1504.

There is in the centre the usual late Perugino erection, under which the scene takes place, and away in the distance is the customary Umbrian landscape. The whole picture is suffused with a delicious, sunny light, and is very pleasing to behold. The fresco is a cherished possession of the city of Città, and its inhabitants are always glad for the great curtains to be drawn back that cover it, in order that they may feast their eyes upon the picture. I cannot, however, refrain from mentioning how touched I was by the exquisite and genuine courtesy of the people of this city, so characteristic as it was of the Italian country-folk. The little crowd that followed me into the oratory seemed to acknowledge possession on my part in the picture for the time being, and begged my permission, with many apologies, that they might look at the fresco which I had paid to have uncovered. They eagerly took me through their town, and pointed out every treasure that they possessed, giving up gladly to me a considerable portion of their day, and only too anxious that I should join with them in admiring the work of their great artist.

To understand the hill towns of Umbria, and to see them in all their peaceful, sunny slumber, a visit must be paid to Città della Pieve. Perugino's works find a more fitting resting-place in his old birthplace than in any place that I know. The town is solemnly quiet and strangely beautiful. It is like a petrified city, suddenly stopped in its growth, left high and dry by the moving waters of civilisation. It is untouched and unspoiled, and the visitor to-day finds the town very much as it was when Perugino left it. It is a city of peace, and the peace glows on the faces of the people. They are the kindest and most courteous of people; many of them look as though they had stepped from the master's pictures: they stand in quiet, meditative postures, and in church kneel in solemn ecstacies of prayer. They are purely a pastoral people, working hard in the day, coming quietly home at night, and full of tender devotion in their religion, of ardent faith, and of deep domestic love in their family circles. The very influence of Perugino's pictures seems still to dwell in this little Umbrian town.

Another little town is Panicale, and here, in the following year, Perugino painted a "San Sebastian." Lo Spagna, his pupil, is said to have lived in this town, and therefore, Crowe suggests, had a hand in the work; but the fresco is signed by Perugino, dated on the columns A.D. MDV., and is thoroughly typical of Perugino's work in every way. There is no need to look for Lo Spagna's hand in the fresco, or to expect it; but it is, of course, quite possible that he assisted Perugino in painting it.

This work is not a true fresco, but *a secco* – that is, it was painted on the dry wall.

The church of San Agostino, in the same town, contains a fresco of the "Virgin and Child," and here the spectator will be safe in attributing the greater part of the work to Lo Spagna.

It was in this year that Isabella d'Este Gonzaga, Duchess of Mantua, commissioned a picture for her boudoir in the Ducal Palace. She gave very definite instructions as to its subject, writing to the artist in the following words: "My poetical idea, which I desire you should paint, is a battle of Chastity against Love – that is, Pallas and Diana fighting against Venus and Love. Pallas must have almost conquered Love; after breaking to pieces the gold arrow and silver quiver that she has cast down before her feet, she holds him with one hand by the bandage that the blind one wears over his eyes, and she raises her other hand to strike him. Between Diana and Venus victory must seem to be doubtful; Venus shall be injured in some part of her dress only; as to Diana, her clothes shall be set on fire by the torch of Venus, but the bodies of the two goddesses shall suffer no wound."

In June 1505, Perugino wrote to the Duchess from Florence, having come there from Panicale, explaining that he had executed her commission in tempera, as he had deemed that to be the best medium in which to depict the scene. He received eighty ducats for the picture, and it remained in the Palace at Mantua La Gloriosa until the time of the plunder in 1630, when it was removed to the castle of Richelieu, where it remained down to the time of the Revolution, and it now hangs in the Louvre. The master was evidently in this picture "cribb'd and confined" by the terms of his commission. His genius was not allowed its own proper development, and he was bound down to certain scenes, which his patron had indicated so precisely. The consequence is, that there is no heart in the picture. It is pleasing in a superficial way; the landscape and the trees are delightful, although the latter are lacking in proportion; but the composition is far too crowded, weak in drawing, and careless in execution.

There is a real sense of movement in it, and its colouring is pleasant; but the closer the picture is scrutinised the less it will be liked; and faults in drawing abound on all hands. Most noticeable of all, perhaps, is the carelessness shown in the sizes of the figures. They are of all heights, some gigantic, and out of all proportion, others far too small and grotesque in shape, and others again, in the middle distance, far too gigantic for their position. There is a skilful bit of movement in the figure of Mercury in the sky, and there is some shrewd originality in the various fables represented in the background; but the picture is far from satisfactory, and not worthy of the master.

A fortnight after he had written to the Duchess he met Lorenzo di Credi at the Duomo in Florence, as the two artists had been called in to decide as to the respective merits of two heads in mosaic intended for the chapel of San Zenobius.

Twice during the master's life was he called upon to complete another man's work, once at S. Severo toward the end of his life, as will be seen later on, and in the year now under consideration for the church of Santissima Annunziata.

An important "Descent from the Cross" had been commissioned by one Jacopo Federighi, a Knight of Malta, for the brethren of SS. Annunziata de Servi, and the instruction given to Filippino Lippi. In 1503 he commenced the work, but in 1505 he died, leaving it half finished, and the monks called in Perugino to complete it, giving him also a commission to paint an "Assumption" of the same size for the reverse of the altar-piece. The first commission he executed well, the second so carelessly that Vasari states that the monks gave the place of honour to the picture begun by Filippino Lippi. Of this picture, now in the Accademia, Lippi did the upper part, Perugino the lower, and it is right to add that he so well blended his work with the work of

Lippi that the picture is harmonious and delightful.

The swooning of The Virgin on the left is not well drawn or pleasingly represented, but the faces are good. The kneeling Magdalen is almost dramatic, while the action of Joseph who is supporting the dead Body as it is removed from the Cross is excellent. Faces, feet, and hands are all good in this picture, those of the two men especially, and in the completion Perugino evidently did his utmost, and succeeded. The "Assumption" is, however, far different. Vasari expressly records the story that "when the picture was first uncovered, all the new artists censured it greatly, principally because Pietro had again adopted the same figures that had been previously painted in other of his works, for which his friends reproached him not a little, declaring that he had taken no pains." Pietro's reply was: "I have painted in this work the figures that you formerly commended, and which then pleased you greatly; if they now displease you and you no longer extol them, what can I do?"

Our artist was, however, only begging the question. His habit of repetition must by that time have been well known and understood. We have already seen how the same figure appears again and again, in somewhat different pose in his pictures, and the fault is a common one, especially in the Umbrian school; but at least the pictures are different in other respects, in arrangement, in grouping, in composition. Here, however, the case is altered. The resemblance between this "Assumption" and the "Ascension" at Lyons, the "Ascension" at Borgo and the "Coronation" at Perugia, is so close as to show that the artist had hardly troubled to make any change. The groups of angel musicians around the mandorla in the "Assumption" and two "Ascensions" are practically identical. The flying angels and cherubs below are also alike, and the changes made in the group of apostles on the ground are but slight. The Virgin who stands beneath the Christ in the "Ascension" is replaced in the "Assumption" by St. Thomas, who stands in the identical pose.

The empty tomb is, of course, introduced; the mandorla is

composed of rays instead of cherubs, and the emblems of St. Peter and St. Paul are omitted; but in general effect the pictures are the same, and the group in the "Coronation" at Perugia, attributed in the catalogue to Perugino, closely resembles the group in the other three pictures. When to all this is added the fact that the "Assumption" is painted in a slovenly way, the landscape hardly more than suggested, the clouds streaky and wooden, and the draperies formal and stiff, it will be seen that the complaint made by both monks and artists was a well-founded one. The picture is certainly charming in general effect and colouring, especially in its present high position over a side altar; but it will not bear inspection, and is no credit to the artist.

He was, however, becoming careless and indifferent to his work, and, growing old, was more sensitive to the remarks of the younger and more popular men. The satirical verses that this latest picture evoked, and the complaints of his patrons and friends, were a cause of constant irritation to him; and although, as Morelli records, he had taken a house, and purchased in this very church, the SS. Annunziata, a burial-place for himself and his descendants, he turned his back upon Florence, and retired in great indignation to Perugia. His name appears no longer on the rolls of the painters' guild in Florence, but in 1506 is again recorded on the similar rolls of Perugia.

A curious feature about this incident is that in the Uffizi appear several drawings and studies which, it is said, were prepared for this very picture. If it were so, it would imply that Perugino took great pains in the preparation of the picture, and made elaborate studies for it. At the first glance a drawing of five apostles, which is the most important of these studies, might readily bear the name attributed to it, but on very close scrutiny, it will be found that it does not exactly or even closely resemble any group in the Annunziata picture, nor in the "Ascensions" at Lyons or Borgo San Sepolcro, nor the "Coronation of Our Lady" at Perugia. It much more closely resembles, and is in parts identical with Perugino's later work at Rome, in the Camera dell' Incendio, and it is for this work that I believe the studies were prepared, which the Uffizi catalogues to the Annunziata picture.

CHAPTER IX

AGE, INFIRMITY, DIGNITY, AND DEATH

Arrived in Perugia, Pietro's first work, as we are told by Mariotti and Orsini, was to collect certain sums of money due to him for pictures he had painted. From the town authorities for the "Cambio" he drew 350 ducats. From Città della Pieve he claimed twenty-five florins, but accepted, on March 29th, 1507, a house from the municipality in settlement of his claim. To the town of Panicale he wrote for payment of the balance due to him for the "San Sebastian," but in his letter made a generous offer to the authorities. Two years before, says Mariotti, he had lent fourteen painted banners to Panicale for a Corpus Christi procession, and he now wrote that the town might, if it desired so to do, keep the banners as a gift from him, but that if that was done he considered he ought to be paid the balance of the eleven florins that was still due to him. The Priori accepted his kindly offer, and on September 1st, 1507, sent him the eleven florins, for which he gave them a receipt, and they accepted his gift of the banners.

An interesting commission reached him in Perugia in 1507. The executors of one, Giovanni Schiavone, a master carpenter, commissioned an altar-piece for Sta. Maria Nuova de Servi, and this commission Perugino executed with great care.

The picture, which now hangs in the National Gallery, is a remarkable one in many ways. The painter was over sixty years old; he had just finished a very poor and slovenly work. He was, a little later, to execute some works even more strange in their stiffness, formality, and want of accurate drawing, but in this picture much of his old fire is to be seen. The colouring is notable, as the picture is full of that living golden haze or glow which marks his finest works, and is so typical of them. It has caught and imprisoned the sunshine, and is forever brightening the room in which it hangs. The composition, too, is original; the two angels in the air do not appear in other pictures. As far as I know never did Perugino, save in this picture, represent the Madonna being crowned by angels, nor did his angels bear palms. In the figure of St. Francis he does not follow his usual type or pose, and the divine Child possesses far more vigour of life, and is far better drawn and proportioned than is generally the case. Is it possible that the master's old studies and cartoons were still in Florence or *en route* for Perugia, and that in their absence he was compelled to design a work of unusual character, and on original lines?

The Schiavone picture completed, Perugino left for Foligno, where a "Baptism of Christ" had been commissioned for the church of SS. Annunziata. It was commissioned by one Giovanni Batista, whose name appears upon it, and who was probably Giambattista Caporali of Perugia, but the church is now disused and neglected, and the fresco is in very damaged condition.

While at Foligno, Perugino received orders to come to Rome. Pope Julius II. desired him to decorate some ceilings in the Vatican, but it is not very clear what the instructions really were. One ceiling we know he decorated, that in the Camera dell' Incendio, because when Raphael completed the decoration of the series of rooms he spared this ceiling out of respect to his old master. The Holy Father, prior to Raphael's arrival in Rome in 1508, had been employing the chief well-known artists of the day in his schemes; Piero della Francesca, Bramantino, Sodoma, Luca

Signorelli, and others had received commissions. Raphael, who, then only in his twenty-fifth year, was heard of through Bramante, was summoned to Rome to assist the others, but his work so delighted the Pope that the other artists were dismissed, and Raphael was ordered to destroy their frescoes and to replace them with his own. One, however, of Perugino's ceilings Raphael spared as just recorded.

This ceiling decoration consists of three tondi within borders and decoration of flowing arabesque design, and both composition and figures are marked by the master's early methods, and do not reveal the power of his more mature work. Their composition is more crowded than was Perugino's wont, but the exquisite beauty of the figures is unmistakable, and it was a graceful act on the part of Raphael to spare this fine ceiling as a memorial of his master's work in the Vatican stanze.

Two at least of the Uffizi drawings were prepared, I believe, for this ceiling. What else Perugino did in Rome on this his second visit, or how long he stayed, is not known. We are, however, told that he lodged in the Palazzo San Clemento, that he met Luca Signorelli and Pinturicchio, and that they dined together at Bramante's house, and the scene is described by Giambattista Caporali in his comments on Vitruvius. Perugino at this time introduced his pupil Caporali to the artists in Rome.

Crowe thinks that from Rome Perugino went to Assisi, where, at the church of Santa Maria degli Angeli, on the rear wall of the portiuncula, facing east, he painted a fine "Crucifixion."

Few events in his life show the very high reputation enjoyed by the master more clearly than is shown by this commission. To be called in to decorate the very wall of the sacred little house that in the sixth century had sheltered St. Benedict and in the thirteenth century St. Francis, and which even at that period had become one of the great shrines of Christendom, was honour indeed. The "Crucifixion" somewhat closely resembled the one in the Accademia painted for the monastery of St. Jerome, but hardly anything of the artist's work now remains. The upper part of the fresco was destroyed in 1700 during the demolition of the old choir to make way for the present building, and the lower part which remains was entirely restored by Castellani in 1830. From Assisi Perugino went to Siena and painted a picture for the Vieri family for the church of San Francesco which was completed September 5th, 1510,[*N] and which was burnt in 1655. One fragment only remains of this picture, a face of very considerable beauty, which belongs now to Miss Hertz, and is in her home in Rome.

In Siena, also, Perugino painted a "Crucifixion" for the Chigi altar in San Agostino, for which he was paid 200 ducats. This is still in existence, but is a stiff and formal piece, especially if compared with his earlier renderings of the same dread scene. Two features distinguish it from other crucifixions. The pelican in its piety with its three young in their nest surmounts the Cross, a piece of symbolism used nowhere else by the artist, and the floating angels carry with them double twisted ribbons instead of a single one. Orsini, at this stage, says that Perugino went to Florence, but he was soon back in Perugia (1512), where he purchased two farms and a house.

Mariotti records the transaction. The total sum was 1600 florins, but Perugino could not pay the entire sum at once, and paid down a deposit and gave over a house in Porta Santa Anna which he had received in payment for a picture, and promised to pay other sums at fixed times till he had cleared off the amount.

In this same year we find the wandering artist at the little hill town of Bettona, so difficult of access, and situate near to Assisi, and the pictures which remain in proof of his visit are extraordinary and remarkable ones.

The chief one is a votive picture commissioned by one Boto da Maraglia who had been taken prisoner by the French but released. The picture represents a gigantic figure of St. Anthony, calm and almost expressionless, and then a curious dwarfish figure of Boto, kneeling at his feet, in full armour, gazing up into the face of his patron saint to whom he renders his thanks. The other one is a Madonna, who is also of abnormal size, gathering under her ample cloak kneeling figures of San Manno and San Girolamo, together with much smaller figures of the man and his wife who commissioned the picture. These pictures are in very bad condition, but distinctly interesting, as they differ so much from Perugino's ordinary work. Still journeying around Perugia, we find our artist visiting in 1512 and in 1513 his native town of Città della Pieve.[*O] How long he stayed there is not clear, nor whether he went again and again to the town or remained there for a year or two. There are two pictures at Città dated 1513, another done in 1514, and a fourth in 1517, and a fifth without date. The "Virgin and Child with four saints," St. Protasius, St. Peter, St. Paul, and St. Gervasius, painted for the cathedral of St. Gervasius, is marked by that formal, and, although sweet, yet sickly sentimentality that distinguished much of Perugino's later work. It is terribly formal and stiff, and only detached parts of it, such as the faces of Our Lady, the Child, and St. Peter, are really beautiful.

It was ordered by the Prior, and is signed and dated. The other one in the Duomo, bearing the same date, is of the "Virgin and Child with four saints," and then in a chapel is one of the "Baptism," which clearly belongs to the same period and is as formal and superficial as the other two.

In the church of St. Peter, over the altar, is the picture which was painted in the following year, and is in far better condition than are the other three, and distinguished by a grace that is absent from the others. The face of St. Anthony is benevolent and expressive, but little more can be said in favour of this picture. There is, however, some strength and some tenderness in what remains of the ruined fresco in the church of St. Servi. Nearly all the fresco is gone. Part has been cut away to make a door, part has faded, part has crumbled away, part has been picked off the wall, but what remains is wonderfully beautiful. It is but a fragment, a ruined, faded bit, but it differs entirely from every other "Crucifixion" that Perugino ever painted and is full of graceful figures. The chief part that is left is the group of the holy women assisting the Virgin as she sinks to the earth in a swoon, and it is worth all the journey to Città to see this group. There is life and vigour here, this is real anguish of spirit and bitter grief depicted in the faces, and we do not in the least wonder that not only M. Broussolle, but Mrs. Vaughan and Miss Duff Gordon, who are amongst the few who have penetrated to this remote town and absorbed its spirit and its beauty, speak in words of reverence of the pathos of this scene.

In all his life Perugino never painted anything more tender and sweet than he did at St. Servi in his old home, and the fragment that remains should be guarded with infinite care, for, damaged as it is, it is most precious.

One work only remains that can be definitely attributed to the next year, 1518, and then for two years we know nothing of Perugino, although we are able to surmise as to the work that engaged his time. The 1518 picture was painted in Perugia for the great church of San Francesco al Prato. It represents San Sebastian bound to a column and attacked by archers, and is signed and dated. During the next two years, it may well be imagined that Perugino was hard at work at the great altar-piece for St. Agostino, which had been ordered before 1512.

One of the most puzzling questions which arises in a book about Perugino is how this ancona is to be reconstructed. It is scattered far and wide over Europe, and only important parts of it are now in Perugia.

One altar-piece, which is stated to have come from San Agostino, must have, I think, belonged to another altar and had nothing to do with that double ancona. It represents the Madonna with St. Nicolas, St. Bernard, St. Jerome, and St. Sebastian, and had the space below left for the tabernacle, the mark of which can still be seen.

Perhaps to this same period belongs the fantastic "St. John Baptist, with St. Anthony of Padua, St. Sebastian, St. Jerome, and St. Francis," painted for San Francesco al Prato. The St. Sebastian here has degenerated into a girlish fop, with elaborate head-dress and boots, and although the faces of the other three saints are pleasing and thoughtful, yet the picture is terribly degenerate, and the landscape in the rear hardly exists at all. The same faults are to be found in the typical late pictures to be found at Spello, in the church of Sta. Maria Maggiore. They are both signed and dated, and belong to 1521, and can only be admired for their colour and for the knowledge that even they reveal of the possibilities of space.

The tale of the 1521 pictures is not yet, however, nearly complete, but in the works now coming under consideration an improvement will be perceptible.

The six figures of St. Scholastica, St. Jerome, St. John, St. Gregory, St. Boniface, and St. Martha, which Perugino added in the church of San Severo, below the fresco painted by his great pupil in 1505, are dignified and impressive. They are far removed from the power of early work; there is a cumbersomeness about their draperies, and a sameness in pose and style, but the face of St. Boniface is lovely, and those of St. Jerome and St. John solemn and grand, while all the figures are well-proportioned, and stand well on their feet.

It was a melancholy duty to complete the unfinished and early work of the great pupil who had so far surpassed his master, but evidently the old master did it as well as he could, lingered lovingly over its details, and proudly recorded his name upon his work. The whole fresco is of notable interest, as the combination of the works of master and pupil, with the inscriptions recording the names of the artists and of the patrons who employed them, is unique. Sixteen years had passed since the upper fresco was painted. Raphael had mounted on from glory to glory, leaving behind him all his contemporaries, and had been reckoned as the king of them now; and now, in the year after his death, his old master is called up to complete the work, and he gives to the commission the best abilities of a fading old age.

Perhaps his neighbours commiserated too much with him, or

taunted him with the decay of his powers. Whatever may have been the cause, it is quite clear that, rising superior to the quaintness, stiffness, and formality of Spello, Perugino suddenly wakened up into some old vigour, and much of the old spirit is to be seen in his last works.

In the church of San Francesco at Montefalco is his Presepio, which it is absurd to give to Tiberio d' Assisi, Lo Spagna, or Manni. Works by all these men hang close by in the deserted church, which now forms a wonderful picture gallery, and the comparison can easily be made.

There is a record of a visit from Perugino to the town *en route* for Trevi in this very year, and with him came two at least of these pupils, but no pupil ever painted this Presepio, although it is most probable that the lunette above it is by Tiberio d' Assisi. The lower picture, however, glows with golden sunshine, and the landscape is full of beauty, and represents, as was so often the case, the view to be seen from the very walls of this wonderful old city. Some of the faces are formal, the draperies are coarse and stiff, and show signs of hurried work, but the sense of distance proclaims the author of the fresco, and the faces of St. Joseph and of the Virgin and the dainty decoration of the columns are with the landscape really good pieces of work, and a wonderful improvement upon the pictures at Spello, Bettona, or in the Duomo at Città della Pieve.

Outside Montefalco is San Fortunato, where Tiberio d' Assisi painted the cloisters, and here probably Perugino stopped, and one figure in the ceiling is certainly his work, perhaps done to show Tiberio a suggestion as to the decoration, or put in at the pupil's own request. Then he journeyed on to Trevi, another delightful hill town, full of charm and beauty, and there, an old man of seventy-five, in the church of Sta. Maria della Lacrime, outside the town, he painted his "Adoration of the Magi." It is the old, old design. There is the wooden erection, the enthroned Madonna and Child, the kneeling Magi, the crowd of attendants. In the distance are the servants with horses and camels, and away beyond are the blue hills, the river, and the sky.

Certainly it is degenerate work; but which of the men of his time could do such work? No one else could so present the continuous space of nature, the spaciousness and vastness of the distance, or bathe his pictures in the dreamy sunlight of summer. I lingered long before this fresco, loth to leave it, its tranquillity is so marked, its airiness is so impressive.

It was while completing this picture that the message as to the San Agostino ancona reached Pietro. Back he came to Perugia in 1522, painted the "Transfiguration" for Sta. Maria Nuova, and its three predella panels now in the Perugia Gallery, and the frescoes in the Nunnery of S. Agnese (where he had relations), which I have not been able to see, as the Nunnery is now strictly cloistered.

Three more frescoes only remain for mention. A harsh and hurried one in the cathedral of Perugia, in which the Magdalen's face is the redeeming feature, a faded but lovely "Nativity" in the Alfani Rooms (Room 13) in the Perugia Gallery, which is full of exquisite feeling and tender, reverent grace, and finally, the last and unfinished work which now hangs in the National Gallery. This is a huge fresco transferred to canvas, and measures 19 ft. 6 in. long. It was executed at Fontignano in 1523, and is said to have been the last work of the artist. The hand had not lost its cunning, and there is much of the early sweetness in this huge fresco. There is the charm of its faded blues and purples, the haze of its shimmering sunshine, and the tender reverence of the kneeling figures.

There are just the same accessories as were adopted by Perugino in earlier "Adorations," very much the same grouping, and almost identical figures, and in these respects the two last pictures that the artist painted are almost copies, one of the other, differing only in proportions. The Perugia fresco is small, the London one very large; but both are really lovely compositions, full of mysterious charm, and it is pleasant to know that the artist's last works were not the queer, quaint ones of Spello and

Bettona, but the wonderful, scenes of the "Adoration," painted with much of his old vigour and with all his earlier charm.

Mariotti tells us that Perugino died at the Ospedale of Fontignano, and Orsini suggests that it was of plague. There were various traditions as to his burial; even in Mariotti's time, Vasari states, he was honourably buried at Città della Pieve, but there is absolutely nothing to support this statement. The artist was, according to local account hurriedly buried in a field, as at that time all town funerals were forbidden on account of the violence of the epidemic. In the following year, his sons, desirous of affording him an honourable burial, according to the rites of Holy Church, tried to make arrangement for the removal of the body.

On December 30th, 1524, they entered into a contract with the monks of San Agostino, who were still in their father's debt 50 scudi, that they should remove his body from Fontignano and bury him in their church, and the sons agreed to pay for the Mass. Mariotti says that there was in his time no proof that that ever was done, but the very fact of the contract proves that nothing could be said to the discredit of Perugino's life or character, and refutes idle rumour as to his atheism.

A spot was pointed to Mariotti half-a-mile from Fontignano as the place of Perugino's burial, but he records that, although nothing was found when this spot was examined, yet he could never find any proof that the devout wishes of the three sons, Giovanni Batista, Francesco, and Michel Angelo, were ever fulfilled. It is most probable that owing to the plague and to the war, which at the time were raging in Perugia, the removal of Perugino's body was delayed, and so eventually quite forgotten. No man, therefore, knows where the great artist was buried, and the burial-place he bought at SS. Annunziata in Florence, was unoccupied. Mariotti states that his only descendant was a grandson, one John Battista Vannucci, whose name appeared as a scholar in the University of Città della Pieve. It is, therefore, quite possible that the plague carried off not only the artist, but shortly afterwards his three sons also. Pietro's wife was one Chiare

Fancelli, a very beautiful girl, whom he married, 1st September 1493, in the Canonica in Perugia. She was the daughter of Luca, an architect and surveyor in the service of the Marquis of Mantua. Tradition states that she was the model for the angel with Tobias in the National Gallery. She brought him a dowry of 500 gold ducats, and had in all seven children; and Vasari states that Pietro was exceeding fond of her, and so proud of her beauty that he loved to give her beautiful jewels and costly dresses, and to adorn her with his own hands. After his death she wrote in 1524 to the Marchioness of Mantua offering her a picture by her husband (not now known) of "Mars and Venus discovered together by Vulcan," which was for sale. This information Braghirolli discovered. She was still living in 1540.

Of Perugino's scholars who so closely followed their master, it will suffice just to mention Lo Spagna, Eusebio di San Giorgio, Giovanni Batta Caporali, Tiberio d'Assisi, Giannicola Manni, Rocco Zoppo, Baccio Ubertini, but the glory of Raphael has overshadowed them all.

It may be well finally to review briefly the characteristics of the artist, and of his work. Perugino appears to have been a man of great determination, Lupatelli says of iron will. He had known poverty in his early days, and had faced it. He was determined to push his way and make a living, and, if possible, a great name; and he succeeded in his purpose. Brunamonti speaks several times of his desire to go ahead, and it is quite clear that he was ambitious and energetic, and hence his success. There is no proof whatever that he was irreligious, or, as Vasari implies, atheistic, but his face betokens a mind that would not ordinarily be satisfied without argument and examination, and it was perhaps his controversial habits that obtained for him the character that Vasari has recorded. His employment by the Church, not only by the Chief Pontiff but by numerous dignitaries and by many religious orders, and the arrangement just mentioned and entered into by his sons as to his burial, sufficiently refute Vasari's statements; but beyond this, it is inconceivable that such pictures as the Pazzi

"Crucifixion," the San Severo "Deposition," the Vallambrosan "Assumption," to name but three typical ones, could be painted by an irreligious man. I am disposed to consider his portraits as his finest works, and to me the portraits of the two monks of Vallombrosa reveal him as a great master, very skilful, and possessed of wonderful power.

His more popular compositions are many of them of striking beauty, especially in the delineation of faces, in the landscape, and in the colouring, and, above all, in that wondrous genius for representing open limitless space to which attention was given in Chapter I. Perugino is never dramatic, he is always lyric, and the poetical charm of the Umbrian school is at its very zenith in his hands. He is not passionate, as is Botticelli, nor strong, moving, and forceful as is Signorelli.

The delights of movement, the extremes of rage or desire, did not appeal to him. He was not as diversified as was Lippi; he never reached the stolid impressiveness of Ghirlandajo, nor the ecstatic devotion of Fra Angelico. He was not so purely illustrative as was Pinturicchio, but very far exceeded him both in genius and in power. The emotions of pathos were not beyond his reach, the stateliness of dignity he could represent if he desired, but his charm is in the calm quiet of his pictures, in their tender reverence and exquisite sweetness, in their poetry rather than in their power. His creations are dreamy and contemplative, full of faith, hope, and expectation, and they embody and express the reality of a spiritual world of serene peace and satisfaction which, in its contrast to the world around us, speaks of the revelation of a faith that is true. His execution is masterly, his colouring mystic and glorious, his compositions are complete and united, his sense of decoration is excellent. He was himself sincere in his work, and his pictures therefore embody this sincerity, and their teaching is to lift the soul from sordid thoughts, and to raise it to Heaven itself.

CHAPTER X

SAINT SEBASTIAN

There is a tradition in Umbria that upon two occasions Perugino painted miniatures on vellum, and that these works formed pages in two missals or Books of Hours. Several times the story was repeated to me, in Florence, in Perugia, and in other places, and it appears that at one time manuscript evidence of the fact existed in Rome, and may still exist. Of one of these pages I can give no information, as the most diligent inquiry has failed to identify it; but the other one, the earlier of the two, according to the Roman story, is now in England.

Its history is decidedly a romantic one. The volume to which it belongs was once in the possession of Cardinal Giovanni Girolamo Albani, and from him was called the Albani manuscript. He died in 1591, and the manuscript, which tradition says at one time came into the hands of Clement XI., passed on down to the possession of another Cardinal Albani, Giovanni Francesco, at whose death in 1809 it was sold. A small dealer in curiosities obtained it, and Mr. Denistoune, the great collector, saw it in his shop near the Ghetto in Rome, and bought it for 22 scudi, about £5 sterling. Mr. Denistoune brought the book to England, and offered it, so the family story goes, to the British Museum for £250, but failed to persuade the trustees to purchase it; and so ten years afterwards when he returned to Rome he took the manuscript with him.

Gregory XVI. had by this time died, and the carelessness which existed in his time as to the purchase of art treasures in Rome had become a thing of the past. The new Pontiff, Pius IX., was much more particular, and he was ably seconded by Count Rossi in his endeavour to retain in the Eternal City its chief artistic treasures. Count Rossi heard of the Albani book, and Mr. Denistoune, alarmed for the safety of his treasure, wrapped it up in paper, addressed it to his bankers in London, and, explaining that it was his bank pass-book, gave it over to a lady friend who was leaving for England, to convey to London.

Within three or four days of the lady's departure, the agents of the Vatican called on Mr. Denistoune to demand the surrender of the treasure which had, they declared, been stolen from the Library in the Vatican of Clement XI. Mr. Denistoune declared he had not got the book they wanted and gave them permission to search his house. So accurate had been their information that they went at once to the very place in the bookcase whence the volume had been so lately removed, and, not finding it there, they searched the house from top to bottom.

A charge of theft was then formulated against Mr. Denistoune, and he was taken off to the Castle of St. Angelo, and there confined. Mr. Denistoune, however, at once appealed to the English consular authorities, who quickly gave the police to understand that they had exceeded their powers, and, after two days' imprisonment, Mr. Denistoune was liberated, and at once left for England. The late Earl of Ashburnham then heard of the book, and tried hard to get its owner to sell it to him. At last, in an unguarded moment, Mr. Denistoune cheerily said that years before he had offered it to the British museum for £250, and he should not be content with less than three times that price now. Lord Ashburnham jumped at the figures, produced a bundle of notes, and in a few moments obtained the coveted treasure for £750. Until a year or two ago, the little volume rested at

Ashburnham Place, but it was privately sold quite recently, together with several other fine manuscripts, to Mr. Henry Yates Thompson. It is now in his famous and most wonderful collection, and it is to his kindness that I owe the privilege of handling and describing the book. The story has been pieced together from several narratives told me in Italy.

There are four splendid illuminated pages in the volume, each by a different hand, and each page the work of some great artist at his very best. There are also borders and other illuminations, which are probably the work of yet a fifth miniaturist.

The Perugino page is signed:

PETRVS PRVSINVS PINXIT,

and represents Saint Sebastian fastened to an upright pillar of wood, and being shot at by two archers.

These archers are gaily dressed: one, wearing a cap, has long red stockings, brown shoes, and a blue vest and a brown drapery around his waist; the other, who is bareheaded, has blue stockings, yellow boots, a red vest, and green drapery around his waist.

Above, in the air, are two angels, one of whom is turning towards the martyred saint. One angel has a drapery of puce, with green sleeves, and has yellow wings; the other wears orange, with red sleeves, and has green wings. The drapery around Saint Sebastian is puce colour. In the distance is a lovely typical Perugino landscape, extensive, and full of light and air; there are hills and rocks, trees and water, exquisitely painted, and revealing, in their wonderful effect of never-ending distance, the best work of the artist. The silhouetted effect of the trees is particularly characteristic. Above is the lofty dome of blue sky, bearing upon it the strange, frilled, fleecy clouds in which the artist so delighted, and illuminated by the glow of light that he was so easily able to produce.

The work I attribute to the 1500-1523 period, as the puce colour, the colouring of the angels' wings, and the shape of the clouds, all are characteristics of that period, as well as the subject itself and its treatment.

It is important to refer briefly to the way in which Perugino painted Sebastian. There are: 1. the Cerqueto fresco of 1478; 2. the Fiesole picture, now in the Uffizi, of 1493; 3. the Wantage figure, of about 1498; 4. the Borghese picture, of about 1500; 5. the Panicale fresco, of 1505; 6. the Perugia fresco, of 1518; 7. the manuscript in question; and the drawing of an archer at Christ Church, Oxford. (I leave out of this consideration the effeminate St. Sebastian, in the Perugia gallery, Sala XI., No. 16.)

The Cerqueto one, and all the others save No. 2, represent St. Sebastian tied to a column of wood; but the Cerqueto fresco is far more robust in its delineation, more Signorellesque in its muscular power than any of the others. The bend of the neck and the upward gaze of the face are distinctive of all seven.

The Uffizi picture alone (2), in which St. Sebastian is one of the two attendant saints, standing one on either side of the enthroned Madonna, represents the figure with his hands, as usual, bound behind him, but he is not bound to a column. In Nos. 2, 3, and 4 the saint stands on the ground; in the others, 1, 5, 6, and 7, the wooden post is elevated above the ground. The position of the feet differs in every case, but in each instance the face is upturned, the hands bound behind the back, the body nude, save for a loin-cloth, and the flesh pierced by arrows. In No. 7 there is but one mark of an arrow to be noted. The page in question most closely resembles the Perugia picture, No. 6. This came from the church of San Francesco al Patro, and was painted in the year of a great visitation of plague, and the selection of the plague saint is thus accounted for. In this picture there are the two archers only (whereas at Panicale there are four), and there are the two angels, which in the Panicale fresco certainly appear, but are in attendance upon the Eternal Figure, whose representation appears in the lunette above. One angel in the Perugia picture (6) bears a crown. It is impossible to say what the other one carries, as the fresco is so damaged; but the colouring of these angels very closely resembles the gay colouring in the manuscript. The column was a very persistent type, as in structure the one painted in 1478 appears over and over again later on. The column in this manuscript very closely resembles the central limb of Perugino's crosses in his crucifixion scenes; and in this detail Lord Wantage's picture resembles most closely the manuscript; but the landscape, which is but slight and loose in this picture, is very fine in the manuscript and almost identical with the Città della Pieve landscape, and with the Bettona one, and closely resembles the repainted Borghese picture (4), which has also the frilled clouds that are so distinctive in the manuscript.

Mr. Thompson's manuscript is in perfect order, and is a most beautiful work. I have no hesitation in accepting it as a genuine work of Perugino, and the very folds of the drapery, when compared with the same arrangement in other pictures, will be found to ratify the attribution.

Comparison with the Perugia fresco (6), will give the probable date of the manuscript, and will afford a striking example of the readiness with which Perugino used over and over again the same theme, treated in the same manner, varying each representation in some slight, characteristic way, and yet preserving the same general effect which had pleased him so much in days gone by.

CATALOGUE OF
THE WORKS OF PERUGINO

AUSTRIA-HUNGARY.

VIENNA, PICTURE GALLERY.

The Baptism of Christ. Panel. 0·29 x 0·22 = 11 in. x 8 in. [24.]

St. John Baptist is pouring water from a shell upon the head of Our Lord, who stands with His feet in the river Jordan. Near by are two kneeling figures.

This closely resembles the same scene in the cathedral at Città della Pieve, and is probably a copy.

From the collection of the Archduke Sigismond at Innsbruck.

St. Jerome. Panel. 0·30 x 0·23 = 1 ft. x 9 in. [25.]

The saint is kneeling before a crucifix. In his right hand he holds a stone, by his side is the lion, and on the ground a cardinal's hat.

From the same collection.

Madonna and Child. 1·86 x 1·44 = 6 ft. 2 in. x 4 ft. 9 in. On paper. [27.]

The Madonna is on a throne holding the divine Child on her knees. On the right stand St. Jerome and St. Peter, and on the left St. John the Baptist and St. Paul.

On the throne is inscribed: PRESBITER JOHANNES CHRISTOFERI DETERRENO FIERI FECIT MCCCCLXXXXIII.

Purchased in 1796.

Madonna and Child. 0·85 x 0·62 = 2 ft. 10 in. x 2 ft. [32.]

The divine Child, who is on the Virgin's knees, is in the act of imparting a benediction. Behind the Madonna are two female saints.

The picture is signed: PETRVS PERVSINVS PINXIT.

LICHTENSTEIN GALLERY.

Nativity.

A Tondo of the Virgin kneeling before the divine Child, who is seated upon a sack and supported by an angel. Signed: PETRVS PERVSINVS P.

This closely resembles the picture in the Pitti.

BELGIUM.

BRUSSELS, ROYAL PICTURE GALLERY.

Madonna, Christ and St. John. Oval, 0·69 x 0·60 = 2 ft. 3 in. x 2 ft. [477.]

The Virgin is seated upon a stone bench and holds on her knees the infant Christ, who is turning toward St. John.

This picture was at one time in the collection of the Princes of Conti in Florence. It was sold in 1850 to M. P. Vellati of Rome, and from him purchased with two pictures by Crivelli for the Gallery in 1862.

BRITISH ISLES.

LONDON, NATIONAL GALLERY.

Virgin and Child and St. John. Panel. 2 ft. 2 in. x 1 ft. 5 in. [181.]

The divine Child stands erect on a stone balustrade supported by the hands of the Madonna, who is by His side, and playing with a lock of her hair. St. John stands on the ground and has clasped hands and gazes in adoration at the Christ.

This picture, which is painted in tempera, was obtained by the late Mr. Beckford in Perugia, and purchased of him for the Gallery in 1841.

On the hem of the mantle of the Virgin is inscribed: PETRVS PERVGINVS.

The Virgin adoring the Divine Child. Panel; centre 2·1 x 4·2. Side panels, each 1·10 x 4·2. [288.]

The left panel is inscribed below: PETRVS PERVSINVS PINXIT.

These three panels were originally in the Certosa di Pavia.

These three panels were purchased from the Certosa by one of the Melzi family in 1786, and bought of Duke Melzi of Milan for the Gallery in 1856.

The Virgin and Child and two Saints. Panel. 6·0 x 4·11. [1075.]

This picture was ordered of Perugino by the testamentary executors of Giovanni Schiavone, a master carpenter of Perugia, in 1507, and was executed within that year, when it was placed over the altar of their chapel in S. Maria Nuova (de' Servi) in an elaborate carved but ungilt framework, said to be designed by Pietro himself. After the demise of the executors and their heirs the chapel reverted to the Frati Serviti, owners of the church, who subsequently sold the chapel with its contents to the Cecconi family, at whose extinction it was inherited by the family della Penna.

In 1822 Baron Fabrizio della Penna removed the picture to his palace in Perugia, leaving the frame *in situ*, in which at the same time was inserted a copy on canvas executed by a young Perugian painter, Giuseppe Carattoli.

The picture was purchased for the National Gallery from the Baron della Penna in 1879.

The Baptism of Our Lord. Panel, 1·0 x 1·11. [1431.]

St. John the Baptist in the centre of the picture is pouring water from a cup on the head of the Saviour, who stands with His feet in the river. Two angels kneel to the right and two to the left, and behind them again stand four of the disciples, two on either side.

See Chapter I. as to this picture, which I cannot accept as a work of Perugino. It is painted in oil upon an unprepared panel.

Bought in Rome in 1894 for £400.

The Adoration of the Shepherds. Fresco transferred to canvas. 8·2 x 19·5. [1441.]

In the centre the infant Christ lies, supported by a cushion on a purple drapery on the open ground. Behind is a shed surrounded by a fence, within which cattle are lying. On the right and left kneel the Holy Virgin and St. Joseph, and behind them the shepherds approach with offerings. An angel is on either side in the sky.

This fresco was removed from the church at Fontignano in 1843, and is said to be the last work of the painter.

It was purchased by the South Kensington Museum in 1862 from Mr. W. B. Spence of Florence, and is now lent to the National Gallery.

BRITISH MUSEUM.

Study for the figures of Tobias and the Angel. Brown and green.

Study for the Head of a bearded Saint or Prophet. Black and white on brown.

Study for a Virgin and Child.

Study for an angel playing on a Violin.

Study of a Female Saint kneeling with clasped hands (and draperies).

Her head-dress is twisted, and there is embroidery on her robe. Brown heightened with white.

Study for an Adoration of the Magi.

Study for a Pietà.

There are two other drawings labelled Perugino which I cannot accept, and one in the Malcolm collection which is of Perugino's school.

CHRIST CHURCH, OXFORD.

A large finished pen drawing representing the Deposition of Our Lord, in the Pitti Gallery 164.

A Study of an Archer.

A bistre pen drawing for the St. Sebastian at Panicale.

A Study for the Archangel and Tobias, in the picture No. 288 in the National Gallery.

WINDSOR CASTLE COLLECTION.

Study for a figure of the Sleeping Disciple, in the Mount of Olives picture in the Accademia, Florence.

A pen drawing in bistre.

Study for the figures of two Sleeping Disciples for the same picture.

A pen drawing in bistre.

Study of a Female Head.

Bistre heightened with white.

Study for the Armour of the figure of St. Michael, in the picture No. 288 in the National Gallery.

Study of a Female Head.

Attributed to Perugino.

Study for the Fresco in the Sistine Chapel in the Vatican of the Delivery to St. Peter of the keys.

F. A. WHITE, Esq., QUEEN'S GATE, S.W.

The Resurrection. Panel. 10 x 17. Old Masters, 1892. No. 154.
Christ standing upon the open tomb bearing a banner in his left hand.
Around, four soldiers, three sleeping and the fourth moving away in an
attitude of surprise.
From the Dudley Collection.

CAPTAIN G. L. HOLFORD, C.I.E., DORCHESTER HOUSE.

Virgin and Child. Panel. 19 x 13.
The Virgin is seated, having the divine Child, who is nude, erect upon
her knees.

LORD WANTAGE, V.C.

St. Sebastian and St. Jerome. Two Panels each. 17 x 7. Old Masters,
1886. No. 197.
St. Sebastian is bound to a tree, and St. Jerome stands erect with a
stone in his hand, and behind him is a lion.
From an altar-piece.

L. HARDY, Esq., M.P.

Saint in Prayer. Panel. 31 x 11.
Figure of a saint to the left with clasped hands.

LORD ALDENHAM, ST DUNSTAN'S, REGENT'S PARK, N.W.

Virgin and Child. Panel. 13 x 11. Old Masters, 1886. No. 176.
The Virgin is seated, and has the divine Child on her knees, and she is
holding His left hand.

LORD BATTERSEA, SURREY HOUSE, MARBLE ARCH, W.

Head of a Saint. Panel. 13 x 10.
Bust facing, black dress with gold edging.

THE EARL OF DUDLEY'S COLLECTION.

There were exhibited at the Old Masters Exhibition in 1892, five panels, each 10? x 18, Nos. 146, 147, 148, 154, 155, representing "The Nativity," "The Baptism," "Christ and the Woman of Samaria," "The Resurrection," and the "Noli me Tangere."

Originally in the Barker collection, No. 154 now belongs to Mr. F. A. White (q.v.); the others have not been traced.

WILLIAM DRURY-LOWE, Esq., LOCKO PARK, DERBY.

Virgin and Child with Saints. Canvas. 47 x 45. Old Masters, 1893. No. 164.

The Virgin is seated, with the divine Child, who is nude, erect on her knees. His right hand is raised, and in his left is a globe.

On the left is St. Jerome reading a book, and behind him St. Nicolas of Tolenteno. On the right, St. Catherine and a bishop in adoration.

This is now ascribed by Dr. Richter to Lo Spagna, one of Perugino's pupils. The identical picture, executed in fresco, is to be found at Spoleto, and is there considered to be Lo Spagna's masterpiece.

The above easel replica came from the Palazzo Darino at Milan, and was bought in 1852 from Sig. Giovanni Locarnos.

PICTURES AT ONE TIME IN ENGLAND.

C. and C. describe a "Resurrection," in their time belonging to Lord Taunton, and originally in Venice. Signed: SEPVLCRVM CHRISTI PETRVS PERVSINVS PINXIT.

They also refer to a "Virgin and Child between St. Jerome and St. Peter," once at Manchester, originally at Lucca, and latterly in the Northwich collection.

FRANCE.

BORDEAUX, PICTURE GALLERY.

Virgin and Child enthroned with S. Jerome and four Angels, from St. Agostino, Perugia.

This has never been photographed.

CAEN, MUSEUM, HOTEL DE VILLE.

St. Jerome. On Panel. 0·90 x 07·4 = 3 ft. x 2 ft. 5 in. [4.]

This is probably one of the figures of saints that surrounded the great altar-piece at St. Agostino, in Perugia; others at Nantes, Toulouse, Lyons, and Grenoble. Signed: PETRVS PERVSINVS PINXIT.

The saint is kneeling before a Cross, a lion is close by, and on a tree in the centre of the picture is a large red hat.

CHANTILLY.

Study for the Head of an Old Man with a beard and wearing a turban.

GRENOBLE, MUSEUM.

SS. Sebastian and Apollonia, from the great altar-piece painted for St. Agostino, at Perugia.
See Caen, Lyons, Nantes, and Toulouse for other panels.

LILLE, PICTURE GALLERY.

The Chevalier Wicar collection of Old Master drawings contains:
Drawing for the Adoration of the Magi, from the picture in the Museum of Rouen. 0·207 x 0·283. [546.]
In silver paint on prepared paper.

LYONS, PICTURE GALLERY, HOTEL DE VILLE.

The Ascension.
It formed part of a large altar-piece painted in 1495 for S. Pietro in Perugia. The lunette belonging to it is in St. Gervais, Paris, the predella at Rouen; and of the pilaster panels three are at the Vatican and five remain at S. Pietro.

The Eternal Father is above within a circular glory of rays issuing from a cloud. Our Lord rises toward Him pointing upward with both hands. There are angels playing on instruments on either side of Christ, and below on the ground are the Madonna, St. Peter, St. Paul, and the rest of the Apostles.

Given to the town by the French Government and confirmed by Pius VII. in 1816.

SS. Herculanus and James.
Probably from St. Agostino, Perugia.

See Caen, Nantes, and Grenoble for others.

MARSEILLES, PICTURE GALLERY.

The Family of St. Anne, or the Infant Saviour with His five Cousins.

The Madonna is enthroned, with the divine Child on her knees, and St. Anne stands behind her and places her hands on the shoulders of Our Lady. St. Simon and St. Thaddeus are on the steps of the throne playing one with the other. To the right St. Mary Cleophas holds St. James the Less in her arms, and St. Joseph has St. Joseph Justus standing beside him and holding a stick. To the left is St. Mary Salome with St. John in her arms. St. Joachim is behind her, and St. James is standing near by. Each of the saints, including St. Anne but excluding the Madonna and Child, bears its name in the halo around the head. St. Joseph Justus is nude, as is also Our Lord, the other five children have slight draperies about them. The throne is inscribed: PETRVS DE CHASTRO PLEBIS PINXIT.

An original drawing for this picture belongs to the Duke of Northumberland, and is at Alnwick Castle.

NANTES, PICTURE GALLERY.

Isaiah and Jeremiah. Circular pictures. 1·27 diam. = 4 ft. 3 in. [202 and 203.]

Each picture has an inscription on it. On Isaiah are the words ELEVATA E MAGNIFIC?ETIA TVA SVP CELOS D?S; and on Jeremiah CŒLVM SEDES MEA, TERRA AVT?E SCABELL? PED? MEORVM.

Probably from St. Agostino, Perugia.

See Caen, Lyons, Toulouse, and Grenoble for others.

Adoration of Christ. 1·6 x 1·18 = 5 ft. 4 in. x 3 ft. 11 in. [87.]

The Madonna and St. John with two angels are kneeling and adoring the divine Child, who is on a pillow on the ground and has his hand raised in benediction.

The signature is much damaged, and only reads: PETRVS PERVSI PINXIT.

From the gallery of the Count de Brissac, and given to the Gallery of Nantes by the State in 1803.

PARIS, THE LOUVRE.

Virgin and Child. Panel, circular. 1·51 diam. = 5 ft. [1564.]

The Madonna is seated on a throne and has the divine Child on her knees. St. Rosa is on her left, St. Catherine on her right. Behind are two angels, with clasped hands in adoration. The dress of the Virgin is cut square at the neck and fastened with a beautiful brooch. The usual Umbrian landscape is in the background with clearly defined trees.

Once in the Collection Lapeyrière and then passed to the King of Holland, from whom in 1850 it was bought for 53,302 francs.

The Holy Family. 0·80 x 0·66 = 2 ft. 8 x 2 ft. 2 in. [1565.]

The Virgin is seated, and holds the divine Child, who is in the act of benediction, in her arms. On one side of The Virgin is St. Joseph, and on the other St. Catherine of Alexandria. The faces of the Virgin and St. Catherine closely resemble one another. St. Catherine's name is inscribed on her dress, and the picture is signed: PETRVS PERVSINVS PINXIT.

Collection of Louis XVIII. Purchased of M. Scitivaux.

A replica is at Vienna, but in that picture St. Agnes is depicted in lieu of St. Joseph.

See Frankfort.

St. Paul. Circular. 1·02 diam. = 3 ft. 4 in. [1566.]

The saint is standing, his right hand holding the hilt of his sword, and his left hand resting on his side. Behind is a stone balustrade.

St. Sebastian. [1566A.]

This picture was obtained in 1896 from the Sciarra Colonna Gallery.

It is inscribed: SAGITT?E TV? INFIX? SVNT MICHI.

A Combat between Love and Chastity. 1·56 x 1·92 = 5 ft. 2 in. x 6 ft. 4 in. [1567.]

This picture was executed for Isabella d'Este, Duchess of Mantua, and at a later time belonged to Cardinal Richelieu.

Apollo and Marsyas. 0·39 x 0·29 = 1 ft. 3 in. x 11 in. [1509.]

This picture is known under the designation of the Raphael of Morris Moore, from the name of the collector who was the first to definitely attribute its origin to Raphael.

Morelli attributes it to Perugino. See Chapter VI.

It was purchased by the Louvre in 1883.

ROUEN, NEW MUSEUM.

Three Small Pictures, forming the predella of a large altar-piece formerly at San Pietro in Perugia, and painted for the church in 1495. They represent the "Adoration of the Magi," "The Baptism," and "The Resurrection." (472, 3, 4.) The centre piece of the altar-piece is at Lyons, five of the side panels of saints are still at S. Pietro, Perugia, *in situ,* and the three remaining side panels in the Vatican. The lunette is at St. Gervais in Paris.

Given by the State to Rouen in 1803.

TARBES (PYRENÉES), PICTURE GALLERY.

Saint Lawrence. Life size. Panel.
Virgin and Child. Small panel.

TOULOUSE, PICTURE GALLERY.

St. John the Evangelist and St. Augustine.
Probably from St. Agostino, Perugia.
See Caen, Lyons, Nantes, and Grenoble for others.

GERMANY.

ALTENBERG, LINDENAU COLLECTION.

C. and C. describe a picture of "St. Helen," and one of "St. Anthony of Padua," probably sides of the altar-piece at SS. Annunziata de Servi in Florence.

DRESDEN, ROYAL PICTURE GALLERY.

St. Crispin. $0.36 \times 0.25 = 1$ ft. 2 in. x 10 in. [22.]
A fragment on panel.

FRANKFORT, STAEDEL GALLERY.

Virgin and Child with St. John. $0.68 \times 0.52 = 2$ ft. 3 in. x 1 ft. 8 in. [16.]
This picture very closely resembles "The Madonna and Child" at the Borghese Gallery, Rome, also the one at Munich, and also the one in the

Louvre, but neither are replicas one of the other, and each differs in important details.

The groups at Frankfort, Rome, and Munich are evidently, however, painted for the face of the Madonna from the same model.

All four I consider to be genuine but late works.

Bought in 1832 in Munich.

LEIPZIG, MUSEUM.

The Archangel St. Michael.

The angel is standing upon the dragon whom he has just killed with a great sword. The landscape at the back appears to be the work of the master, but the rest of the picture is school work.

MEININGEN, DUCAL PALACE.

M. Berenson states that there are in this collection a "St. John Baptist," and a "St. John Evangelist," by Perugino; but I have not seen them.

MUNICH, OLD PINACOTHEK.

Vision of St. Bernard. Panel. 1·73 x 1·65 = 5 ft 9 in. x 5 ft. 6 in. [1034.]

Formerly in the Nasi Chapel of the Church of St. Spirito, in Florence. Acquired for King Ludwig I. in 1829 or 1830 from the House of Capponi in Florence. There is a study for it in the Uffizi 252, 1115.

Lippo Lippi, Filippino, and Fra Bartolomeo all took the idea from this picture.

The Virgin adoring the Child. Panel. 1·95 x 1·56 = 6 ft. 6 in. x 5 ft. 2 in. [1035.]

The Virgin is standing with clasped hands. The Child is on the ground before her. On the left is St. John the Divine, on the right St. Nicholas.

This picture was taken from Venice to London, thence it came into the possession of Mr. Henry of Paris, where, in 1815, it was bought by Von Dillis for 18,000 francs.

Morelli says this is late and superficial in conception, drawing, and execution.

Madonna and Child. Panel. 0·83 x 0·64 = 2 ft. 9 in. x 2 ft. 1 in. [1036.]

The Virgin is seated, and the divine Child, who is nude, is upon her knees.

Acquired in Florence in 1831 by King Ludwig I., and by the State from the King in 1850.

See Frankfort.

Morelli says this is feeble and overcleaned.

The Baptism of Christ. 0·30 x 0·30 = 1 ft. x 1 ft. [1037.]

The Saviour stands in the shallow water with St. John, who holds his cross in his left hand and in his right the baptismal shell. Two angels stand near by.

The Resurrection. 0·30 x 0·40 = 1 ft. x 1 ft. 4 in. [1038.]

The Saviour stands by the tomb, near which two watchers are asleep; a third is running away.

Two predella pictures from the estate of Inghirami in Volterra, and sold to the Crown Prince in 1818.

Morelli unites with C. and C. in ascribing them to Perugino.

STRASSBURG.

There was at one time in the Picture Gallery, a portion of the great altar-piece of 1521 painted for the church of St. Agostino, in Perugia, but it was destroyed in the conflagration of August 25th, 1870.

It represented the Madonna, but was at one time labelled as St. Apollonia. It was opposite to the archangel in the original altar-piece, and was a tondo.

STUTTGART, ROYAL MUSEUM.

The Nativity. 87 x 87. [236.]
Signed: PETRVS PERRVSINVS.

ITALY.

CHURCH OF ST. MARY OF THE ANGELS, ASSISI (near).

A fragment of a Crucifixion resembling No. 57 in the Accademia. The upper part was destroyed in 1700 during the demolition of the old choir, the lower part was restored by Castellani in 1830.

It is on the Portiuncula on the outside of the east wall.

ASCOLI.

Eastlake states that in a private collection at Ascoli is a "Virgin and Child surrounded by saints," brought from Mentone, near Città di Castello, the upper part of which is in gold with reliefs of angels. If this is so it is quite different to anything else of Perugino's work.

BETTONA, CHURCH OF THE MINORITES.

A votive portrait, commissioned by a Perugian captain called Boto da Maraglia, who was taken prisoner by the French, but eventually released. 6·3 x 4·6 = 2 ft. 1 in. x 1 ft. 6 in.

It is in distemper on canvas, and Boto, in full armour, is kneeling and looking up to St. Anthony, who holds in one hand a book, and in the other the fire.

The inscription is as follows: BOTO DE MARAGLIA DE PEROGA QVANDO FO PREGIONE DE FRANCIOSE CHE FO ADI XI DE FEBRAIO MDXII PETRVS PINXIT DE CASTRO PLEBIS.

In the same church is a Madonna between St. Manno and St. Jerome, with male and female patrons under her cloak, and with angels above. 6·3 x 4·6 = 2 ft. 1 in. x 1 ft. 6 in.

BOLOGNA, PINACOTECA.

The Assumption. Circa, 1496.
Signed: PETRVS PERVGINVS PINXIT.

BOLOGNA, CHURCH OF ST. MARTINO MAGGIORE.

The Virgin in Glory.

The Virgin is in the sky, standing, a child-angel is on either side, and around are cherub heads, while on either side are two kneeling angels. Below are the apostles grouped around the empty tomb. There are two trees, one on either side of the picture, clearly defined against the sky.

BORGO SAN SEPOLCRO, THE CATHEDRAL.

The Ascension of Christ.
This picture, according to Vasari, was painted in Florence, and

commissioned by the Abbot Simone de' Graziani, and conveyed to the cathedral at heavy cost on the backs of porters. There is a similar picture at Lyons very closely resembling this one.

There is a Study for three apostles in this picture in the Uffizi [251, 406.]

CANTIANO, CHURCH OF STA. MARIA DELLA COLLEGIATA.

The Holy Family.

CERQUETO.

Figure of San Sebastian.
The inscription recorded by Orsini ("Vita di P.P." p. 204) is as follows:

S popul de Cerqueto a fatta fare questa capella A.D. Maria Madalena per C.H. da peste gi usci liberare Cavandoli da le Hoscie D tal pena cusigli piaccia cuq HV operare che mi e semp ne abbia ad scampare e tutti qlli C.H. in lei AN devotion AD laude di Dio quisto sermone Petrus Perusinus pinxit MCCCCLXXVIII.

CITTÀ DELLA PIEVE, SANTA MARIA DE BIANCA.

Fresco. About 18 x 18.
The Madonna is seated on a throne under the usual open-roofed canopy, and bears the Infant Christ on her knees. Behind her are the cattle, and at her side St. Joseph with his staff. Two of the kings are kneeling and presenting their gifts. The third is bringing his in. Around are their companions and attendants, and in the background their retinue of horsemen. There is an angel flying toward the canopy, and below it is the star.
The picture is inscribed: A.D. MDIIIJ.

CITTÀ DELLA PIEVE, CHURCH OF ST. PETER.

St. Anthony. Fresco.
St. Anthony seated on a throne, one hand resting on a staff, the other raised in benediction. He is between St. Paul the Hermit and St. Marcellus (or Macarius), who stand beside him. High up above is the Eternal Father

within a mandorla of cherubs.

CITTÀ DELLA PIEVE, THE CATHEDRAL.

Behind the High Altar – Virgin in Glory.
The Madonna is adored by St. Protasius, St. Peter, St. Paul, and St. Gervasius, and the two Umbrian saints carry flags in their hands which bear the arms of Città della Pieve.
The picture was ordered in 1513 Marchisino Cristophori Mansii, prior of St. Gervasio.
It is inscribed: PETRVS CRISTOFERI VANVTII DE CASTRO PLEBIS PINXIT MDXIII.

First chapel on left – Baptism of Christ by St. John.

St. John is pouring the water from a shell over Our Lord's head. Two angels stand by, and above is the Dove of the Holy Spirit.
Right of High Altar – Virgin and Child seated on a throne, with St. John Baptist, St. John Divine, St. Domenic, and St. Francis. (Dated 1513.) Two angels are above.

CITTÀ DELLA PIEVE, ST. MARIA DE SERVI.

A fragment of a Descent from the Cross, in which the Madonna is supported by two Maries.
It is dated 1517. The inscription is much mutilated, and seems to read something as follows: ...... esta hopera fero depengere la campagnia della S .... Cossi dicta in li anno dmi MDXVII Petr P P.

CORCIANO.

The Assumption of the Virgin.
St. Thomas is below between two groups of the other disciples receiving the girdle of Our Lady.
In the Sacristy of the Church are the two predella panels representing the "Adoration of the Magi" and "The Annunciation."

CREMONA, CHURCH OF ST. AGOSTINO.

The Virgin with St. James and St. Augustine.
The Virgin is on a throne, and holds the divine Child in her arms. On

the left is St. James, on the right St. Augustine.

On the throne is inscribed: PETRVS PERVSINVS PINXIT MCCCCLXXXXIIII.

DERUTA

Frescoes are attributed to Pietro by Orsini at this place, but I was unable to find out where they are, and think that they must have disappeared.

FANO, CHURCH OF STA. MARIA NUOVA.

The Annunciation. (2nd chapel.)
The angel, holding the lily, is kneeling before Our Lady, who turns to leave him and with uplifted hands expresses bewilderment at his message. Above, the Eternal Father, seated within a circle of cherubs, looks down in love upon the Madonna. The Holy Ghost as a dove is flying toward the Virgin. The inscription is much mutilated and reads as follows: S.A.T. .... CALE .... TTI QVE PATRVI OLIM PON .... ENERII HAC TABVLA ER ... GI IN .... OHC .... TVRA A .... VII MCCCC .... III PETRVS DE C .... TRO PL. ......

The Virgin and Child. (3rd chapel.)
Our Lady is seated on a throne in the midst under a vaulted portico, and holds the divine Child in her arms. Around are six saints, St. John, St. Francis, St. Peter, St. Paul, St. Mary Magdalen, and a bishop.

The lunette represents "The Resurrection," the predella "The Birth of the Virgin," "The Presentation," "The Marriage," "The Annunciation," and "The Assumption."

A mutilated inscription on the throne reads: dvrantis phanen ad intemerate Virginis lavd? tercentv?m avreis alq hvjvs templi Bono cent? svperaditis hanc solerti cvra fieri demandavit Matteo de Martinotiis fidei commissario procvranti mcccc 97 petrvs pervsinvs pinxit.

FOLIGNO, CHURCH OF LA NUNZIATELLA.

The Baptism of Christ. Circa 1507.
Our Lord is being baptised by St. John. Four angels stand around watching, and in the air are two other angels and seven cherubs. The Holy Ghost is descending in the form of a dove. High above in the curve of the archway is the Eternal Father holding the globe in one hand and with the

other upraised in benediction. On either side are kneeling angels, and around are cherubs.

The inscription between the picture and its lunette is hardly visible, but appears to be DEO ET BEATO JOANNI BATTISTAE SACRVM PIETATE JOANNIS BAPTISTE. The date which originally followed the inscription cannot be read.

FLORENCE, THE PITTI PALACE.

Mary Magdalen. Panel, 0·47 x 0·35 = 1 ft. 6 in. x 1 ft. 2 in. [42.]
On the ornament of the dress is inscribed: "Santa Maria Maddalena."

Portrait of a Woman, sometimes called "The Nun." Panel. [140.]
Bought by Ferdinand III. from Marquis Niccoloni.
It has been attributed to Leonarda da Vinci and to Piero di Cosimo.
Morelli says that this picture is the work of Perugino.

The Entombment. [164.]
The picture is signed: PETRVS PERVSINVS PINXIT AD MCCCCLXXXXV.

There are three studies for this in the Uffizi, 255, 411, 412, 413, and a large study for the complete picture at Christ Church, Oxford.

The Adoration of the Infant Christ. Panel, 0·86 x 0·86 = 2 ft. 10 in. x 2 ft. 10 in. [219.]

In the centre of the picture is Our Lady on her knees with clasped hands in the act of adoring the divine Child, who is nude and seated upon a sack and supported by an angel. On the other of the Virgin is the child St. John, kneeling on one knee and also in adoration of the Christ.

FLORENCE, THE UFFIZI PALACE.

Portrait, believed to represent Francesco delle Opere, a Florentine artist, a brother of the celebrated Giovanni Corniole. He died in Venice 1496. [287.]

The portrait is of a man with bushy hair. He has bright eyes, and is clean shaven. He wears a cap on his head and is clothed in a loose soutane. In his hand is a roll bearing these words TIMETE DEVM. The background is an Umbrian landscape.

The picture is inscribed on the back: 1494 D'Luglio Pietro Perugino Pinse Franco del Ope (delle Opere).

Madonna and Child with two Saints. [1122.]

The Virgin is seated on a throne beneath a vaulted archway. She has the divine Child on her knees. At her left stands St. Sebastian; on the right St. John Baptist.

The inscription on the base of the throne reads: PETRVS PERVSINVS PINXIT AN MCCCCLXXXXIIJ.

The picture was painted for the Church of San Domenico at Fiesole.

There are also three studies in the Uffizi for the Pietà in the Pitti.

FLORENCE, THE ACADEMY.

Portrait of Don Biagio Milanesi, General of the Vallombrosan Order. 1499-1500. [17.]

Portrait of Don Baldassare, Monk of Vallombrosa. 1499-1500. [17 bis.]

Christ on the Mount of Olives. 1492-9. [53.]

Painted for the Convent of the Gesuati, in Florence.

The Assumption. [55.]

At the extreme top is the Eternal Father in a circle with adoring angels. Below, in a mandorla, is Our Lady surrounded by a group of cherubs, who, in their arrangement, follow the lines of the mandorla. On either side are standing angels playing on musical instruments, and below are flying angels and cherub faces. On the ground as spectators of the mystery are four Vallombrosan saints:

Cardinal San Bernardo degli Uberti, San Giovanni Gualberto the founder, St. Benedict, and the Archangel Michael.

The picture is signed: PETRVS PERVSINVS PINXIT AD MCCCCC.

This picture was painted for Vallombrosa.

The Crucifixion. [78.]

On one side of the cross stands The Virgin, on the other St. Jerome with his lion.

From the Monastery of St. Jerome in Florence.

The Entombment. [56.]

This picture was also painted (in about 1493), for the Convent of the Gesuati.

The Descent from the Cross. [57.]

The lower part of the picture is Perugino's work, and the background. Nicodemus and Joseph of Arimathæa are on the left. The Madonna, fainting, but supported by the holy women, is on the right, and in the centre at the foot of the cross kneels Mary Magdalen. The three nails are in the foreground placed on the clothes of one of the men.

This picture was begun in 1503 by Filippino Lippi for the brethren of SS. Annunziata de Servi, at the expense of Jacopo Federighi, a Knight of Malta. Upon Filippino's death in April 1504 it was completed by Perugino.

Drawings.
Case 255.
Nos 411, 412, 413.
Study for the "Deposition from the Cross" in the Pitti Gallery. Silver paint in bistre touched up with white, on grey paper.
254.
407.
Five figures turning to the right.
409.
St Francis. Study for figure in picture in SS. Annunziata. Pen and ink.
418.
St. Jerome kneeling.
253.
1307.
Virgin and Child.
1147.
Figure of a young man.
402.
Venus and Cupid. Etching in bistre touched up in white for the Cambio.
1317.
Figure of a monk.
252.
1320.
An angel and a lily.
400.
Pericles. Pen and ink. For the Cambio.
1435.
Figure of a monk.
416.

Head of

1115.

Vision of St. Bernard. Study for the picture at Munich, 1024.

408.

St. Catherine; and on the reverse of it, Four Loves. Pen and ink.

363.

Madonna and Child. Study for the picture at Perugia. Sala XI. 6.

401.

Moses. For the Cambio.

511.

Two figures.

Case 251.

415.

Socrates. For the Cambio.

405.

Group of five Apostles. Study for the Assumption at SS. Annunziata.

417.

The Madonna. Study for the figure in Sta. Maria dei Pazzi.

403.

Three Apostles. Study for the Assumption at Borgo San Sepolcro. Etched in bistre, heightened with white on tinted paper. On the back of 252, 400, is a Christ on the Cross, in silver paint on blue paper. Study for the Sta. Maria de Pazzi picture.

256.

309.

The Cumean Sibyl. For the Cambio.

FLORENCE, CHAPTER-HOUSE OF SANTA MARIA MADDALENA DEI PAZZI.

The Crucifixion. This is a very large fresco in three compartments. Circa 1496.

In the centre is Our Lord upon the Cross, with Mary Magdalen kneeling. In the right division, St. John and St. Benedict. In the left, the Virgin and St. Bernard. Each division is framed by an archway of pillars.

There are studies in the Uffizi for the "Madonna," 251, 417; and for the "Christ on the Cross," 252, 400.

FLORENCE, CHURCH OF SS. ANNUNZIATA.

In the fifth chapel on the left is a Virgin and Child enthroned between

St. John Baptist and St. Francis, much of which was probably painted by the pupils of Perugino.

There is a study for the St. Francis in the Uffizi, 254, 409.

In the seventh Chapel is an Assumption of the Virgin.
The Madonna is in a luminous mandorla of rays and surrounded by angels and cherubs, while below on the ground the apostles and holy women, who are gazing up into heaven.

There is a study for five of the apostles in the Uffizi, 257, 405.

FLORENCE, CHURCH OF LA CALZA.

The Crucifixion.
The Magdalen is at the foot of the cross, and around are St. Jerome, St. Francis, St. John Baptist, and St. Giovanni Columbini of Siena.

FLORENCE, VIA FAENZA.

I am only prepared to accept the general idea of the Cena di Foligno as belonging to Perugino. He may have done the landscape, but I doubt it; and the figures around the table I do not think are his at all. Mr. Berenson, however, accepts part of this work as Perugino's, and dates it very early about 1490.

FLORENCE, ST. SPIRITO WEST WINDOW.

Ascension.
Mr. Berenson states that this is from a design by Perugino.

MACERATA.

Madonna and Child with two Saints.
Only a small part of this is by the master, the remainder is by pupils.

MILAN, POLDI PEZZOLI MUSEUM.

Madonna and Child. Panel. 0·29 x 0·23 = 11 in. x 9 in.
The Virgin is seated, and has the divine Child on her knees. On either side of her is an angel, one having clasped hands and the other with its

hands folded across its breast.

MONTEFALCO, CHURCH OF ST. FRANCIS (NEW PINACOTECA).

The Nativity.

Perugino's favourite structure with a pointed roof resting on four columns occupies the centre of the picture; under it is the divine Child lying upon the ground. The Madonna and St. Joseph are kneeling on either side, and behind them are the shepherds and some cattle. Above, in the curve of the arch, is depicted the Eternal Father seated on the clouds within a mandorla of cherubs heads and on either side are kneeling adoring angels.

NAPLES, NATIONAL MUSEUM.

Madonna and Child. [11.]

Our Lady is seated, and has the divine Child, who is nude, on her knee. The scene is in a rocky valley. On the left is a man on a white horse and three youthful companions, on the right a group of five persons, two of whom hold golden cups in their hands.

NAPLES, DUOMO.

The Assumption. Said to be dated 1460.

This picture was commissioned, so Vasari says, by Cardinal Oliviero Caraffa, who is represented kneeling to the left.

The Madonna is in a mandorla; two angels above are crowning her, and other angels playing on instruments are around. Below are the apostles and St. Paul, and to the left, the Cardinal with St. Januarius.

I have not seen this picture.

PANICALE, LAGO TRASIMENO, CHURCH OF ST. SEBASTIAN.

Martyrdom of St. Sebastian. Fresco.

The saint is bound to a column which stands on a marble throne in the centre of the pavement of an arched Temple. Four archers are engaged in shooting arrows at the Saint. The Eternal Father appears high above, seated within a circle of cherubs and having on either side a kneeling angel.

On the pedestal is P .... DE CASTRO .... and on the four pillars the date A.D. MDV.

There is a study for one of the archers at Christ Church, Oxford.

PANICALE, LAGO TRASIMENO, CHURCH OF ST. AUGUSTINE.

Virgin and Child.

The Madonna is in the sky within a mandorla of cherubs, and has four angels around her playing on instruments. Below are two saints.

Much of this picture is by Lo Spagna.

PAVIA, CERTOSA.

A picture of six divisions of which the central one in the upper tier is alone by Perugino.

It represents the Eternal Father seated, holding the globe in one hand and giving the benediction with the other. Cherub heads are all around the seated figure.

The three panels in the lower tier are now in the National Gallery, London, and copies take their places in the Certosa at Pavia.

On either side of the Perugino panel have now been inserted panels by Borgognone.

The picture is in the second chapel on the left, that of St. Michael the Archangel.

PERUGIA, PINACOTECA VANNUCCI.

The Coronation of the Virgin. [Sala VIII. 24.]

This is a double picture, one side being in this room and the reverse in Sala X. No. 25.

From the church of S. Francesco al Monte.

St. Jerome and St. Mary Magdalen. [Sala X. 1.]

By the side of St. Jerome is his lion, and in the Magdalen's hand is the cup of ointment.

From the church of St. Agostino.

St. Sebastian bound to a column and shot at by two Archers; above are two angels. Dated A.D. MDXVIII. [Sala X. 2.]

From the church of S. Francesco al Prato.

Pietà. [Sala X. 10.]

Our Lord crowned, standing and extending His hands.

This was originally in an altar-piece, the frame of which is in Sala XIII. No. 16, and the place is still empty which the Pietà filled. In the lower part of the frame a picture by Eusebio has been placed.

The Baptism of Christ. [Sala X. 11.]
St. John stands by the side of Our Lord and is pouring the water upon His head. The Holy Spirit as a dove within a circle of golden rays is in the heavens above attended by cherubs and two adoring angels. Two·female saints are on the ground beneath.
From the great altar-piece in St. Agostino.

The Eternal Father seated and surrounded by Cherubs. [6.]
The lunette for above altar-piece.

The Preaching of St. John Baptist. [7.]

The Marriage of Cana in Galilee. [12.]
These are the predella pieces for above altar-piece and its opposite face.

The Adoration of the Magi. [21.]

The Offering of Christ in the Temple. [16.]

The Prophet David. [15.]

The Prophet Daniel. [19.]
These were part of the same altar-piece. The remaining two are at Nantes.

The Birth of Christ. [20.]
This is the reverse side of the St. Agostino altar-piece, "The Baptism of Christ" No. 11 being the other side.

San Lorenzo. [8.]

St. Louis the Bishop. [9.]

San Costanzo. [13.]

A Martyr. [14.]

St. Jerome. [17.]

St. Lucy. [18.]

San Nicola da Tolentino. [22.]

St. Monica. [23.]
These eight saints surrounded the same altar-piece at St. Agostino, and are believed to have been at the corners on either side.

Madonna with the divine Child and Saint. [24.]

The Archangel Gabriel. [26.]
These are also believed to have formed part of the same altar-piece.

A Crucifixion. [25.]
This was the opposite side of the picture in Sala X. No. 2.

The figure of the Crucified Lord is finely carved in wood and laid upon the canvas.
From the church of S. Francesco al Monte.

St. James. [4.]

St. Jerome. [5.]
Deposited by the Sodality of St. Martin.

The Transfiguration. [Sala XI. 2.]
Our Lord is above in the heavens, standing with hands extended, and within a mandorla of cherub heads. Moses and Elias kneel in the clouds, one on either side of the Christ. Below are the three disciples gazing upwards and shielding their eyes with their hands from the blinding splendour of the sight.

The three predella pictures to this altar-piece (which was originally in Santa Maria Nuova) represent "The Annunciation," "The Birth of Christ," and "The Baptism of Christ."

The Virgin and Child. [6.]
There is a study for it in the Uffizi, 252, 363.
Painted in 1497.
Deposited by the Nobile Confraternita di San Pietro Martire.

The Virgin of Consolation. [14.]

The Madonna is seated in the heavens, bearing the divine Child, who is nude, erect on her knees. On either side are adoring angels, and around are cherubs. Beneath, on the ground, kneel San Francesco and San Bernardino praying for the people who stand in a great crowd in the middle distance gazing up to the Madonna. In the extreme distance is a view of Perugia.

Deposited by the Nobile Confraternita della Giustizia.

The Virgin and Child. [15.]

The Madonna is seated in the heavens and has three cherubs under her feet. On either side are kneeling San Niccolo and San Bernardino da Siena. On the ground St. Jerome, with his lion, and St. Sebastian are also kneeling. In the distance is a view of the city of Perugia.

From the church of S. Agostino.

St. John Baptist and four other Saints. [16.]

St. John stands on a mound in the midst and holds his tall cross, and with one hand points to heaven. On his left is St. Anthony of Padua and St. Sebastian, the latter being partly in armour and wearing a fantastic head-dress and holding an arrow daintily in one hand. On the right are St. Jerome and St. Francis.

St. John the Divine. [Sala XII. 4.]

St. Luke the Evangelist. [8.]
These are *attributed* to Perugino in the catalogue.

The Birth of Christ. A lunette. Fresco. [Sala XIII. 51.]

The divine Child is on a cushion on the ground, and near by are the Madonna, St. Joseph, and three shepherds, all kneeling in adoration. The usual wooden square erection occupies the centre of the picture. Some cattle are seen near at hand.

From the east door of the church of S. Francesco al Monte.

PERUGIA, DUOMO.

Virgin and Child and Saints.

The Madonna is seated under a canopy and holds the divine Child, who raises His hand in benediction, in her arms. On the left stands St.

Sebastian holding an arrow, on the right is a female saint kneeling, and behind her stands St. Joseph with his staff.

PERUGIA, CHURCH OF S. SEVERO.

Raphael's first fresco of Our Lord and many Saints, to which Perugino made additions in 1521.

The inscriptions upon it are as follows: RAPHAEL DE VRBINO DOM OCTAVIANO STEPHANO VOLATERANO PRIORE SANCTAM TRINITATEM ANGELOS ASTANTES SANCTOSQUE PINXIT A.D. MDV.; and below with the figures of SS. Scholastica, Jerome, John the Divine, Gregory, Boniface, and Martha: PETRVS DE CASTRO PLEBIS PERVSINVS TEMP. DOMINI SILVESTRI STEPHANI VOLATERRANI A DEXTERIS ET SINISTRIS DIV. CHRISTOPHORAE SANCTOS SANCTASQVE PINXIT A.D. MDXXI.

In the upper part is the Eternal Father, and below is Our Lord seated, and above His head the white dove of the Holy Spirit. On either side and around Him are adoring angels, and near by, seated in two groups, are, on His right three saints, SS. Maurus, Placidus, and Benedict, and on His left three more saints, SS. Romualdus, Benedict Martyr, and John Martyr.

PERUGIA, CHURCH OF S. PIETRO.

Pietà.

The dead body of Our Lord has just been lifted from the tomb by St. Joseph of Arimathæa, who is supporting it in sitting posture on the edge of the tomb. On either side are St. Mary Magdalen and Our Lady, each holding one hand of Christ.

This was originally part of the great altar-piece of St. Agostino.

For other parts see Grenoble, Toulouse, Lyons, Nantes, Strasburg, and the Pinacoteca.

PERUGIA, NUNNERY OF S. AGNESE.

The Eternal Father with SS. Sebastian and Rocu.

Crucifixion, with two Angels, the Virgin, and St. John Baptist.

The Virgin, with two Angels, St. Anthony the Abbot, St. Anthony of Padua, St. Elizabeth of Portugal, St. Elizabeth of Hungary.

Said to have been signed: PETRVS PINSIT 1522.

These cannot be seen as the house is now strictly cloistered.

PERUGIA, COLLEGIO DEL CAMBIO.

Entirely decorated in fresco.

First and third picture. Twelve standing figures in groups of three, each group consisting of a Greek between two Romans.

1. Fabius Maximus, Socrates, Numa Pompilius.
2. Furius Camillus, Pittacus, Trajan.
3. Lucius Sicinius, Leonidas, Horatius Cocles.
4. Scipio, Pericles, Cincinnatus.

Above the first six figures are seated representations of Prudence and Justice, the virtues, illustrated by the philosophers, and on tablets carried by cherubs the following two inscriptions:

QUID GENERI HVMANO PRÆSTAS DEA DIC AGE PRÆSTONE FACIAS QVAE MOX FACTA DOLERE QUEAS SCRUTARI VERVM DOCEO CAUSASQVE LATENTESET PER ME POTERIT NIL NISI RITE GERI.

SI TRIBVS HIS CVNCTOS SIMILES PIA NVMINA GIGNANTNIL TOTO SCELERIS NIL SIT IN ORBE MALI ME CVLTA AVGENTVR POPVLI BELLOQVE TOGAQVEET SINE ME FVERANT QVAE MODO MAGNA RVVNT.

The Rev. H. R. Ware renders these verses in English as follows:

Thy gifts to man, Oh! Goddess, now relate.
"To do, what done, shall bring no bitter fate;
I show where truth lies hid, the causes tell,
Which learned from me thou may'st do all things well."
or, as an alternative, the last line may read
(Whereby the seeker may do all things well.)

"If the good gods make all men like these three,
In the wide world no wickedness would be.
By me the nations grow in war and peace,
Without my worship antient powers decrease."

Another rendering by the Rev. T. C. Robson is very close to the original but is not as melodious and easy as Mr. Ware's.

Speak, Goddess, where thy gift to man appears.
"My gift to prompt to deeds that cause no tears.
Truth to unveil, secrets to learn I teach,
No slave of mine heaven's justice would impeach.
Had heaven made all men like these three
Evil and crime had ceased to be;
I guide both sword and pen to better ways,
Force without me will fall on evil days."

Above the second six figures are similar representations of Fortitude and Temperance, the virtues specially illustrated by the warriors and similar inscriptions thus:

CEDERE CVNTA MEIS PULSA ET DISIECTA LACERTISMAGNA SATIS FVERINT TRES DOCVMENTA VIRI NIL EGO PRO PATRIA TIMEO CHARISQVE PROPINQVISQVAEQVE ALIOS TERRET MORS MIHI GRATA VENIT.
DIC DEA QVAE TIBI VIS MORES REGO PECTORIS AESTVSTEMPERO ET HIS ALIOS CVM VOLO REDDO PARES ME SEQVERE ET QVA TE SVPERES RATIONE DOCEBOQVID TV QVOD VALEAS VINCERE MAIVS ERIT.

Mr. Ware's translation of these verses is very happy:

Three heroes proof infallible have givenThat by my arms all foes are backward driven,I have no fear for country nor for friendsThe king of terror brings to me amends.Goddess, reveal thy might. "I rule the life;Heroes I train by tempering passion's strife:Follow my rule, thy fiery heart restrain,What greater victory canst thou ere attain."

An alternative of these four lines would be,

Oh! Goddess, tell the secret of thy might."I rule the heart, its foaming tides I fight.Follow my rule, the storms of passion bind;So conquering self a greater self you'll find."

Mr. Robson's rendering is as follows:

All things beneath my hand in scattered ruin lie.Witness these three whose might can none deny.My land, my loved ones, ever I defend,And Death, to others Foe, to me is friend.Speak, Goddess, from thy throne.

❖ 161

"Manners my right.To cool men's souls and balance passion's might.With me as guide self-conquest thou shalt learn,Who then will dare that master will to spurn."

The name of each of the standing figures is clearly recorded at his feet.

Between these two great groups on a pilaster is the portrait of Perugino with this inscription: PETRVS PERVSINVS EGREGIVS PICTOR. PERDITA SI FUERAT PINGENDI HIS RETULIT ARTEM;SI NUSQUAM INVENTA EST HACTENUS IPSE DEDIT.

On the end wall are representations of The Transfiguration and Nativity.

In the former Our Lord is in the clouds in a mandorla of rays, and His hands are raised in benediction. On either side kneel Moses and Elias, and in the sky are the words: HIC EST FILIVS MEVS DILECTVS. On the ground gazing up, but shading their faces from the glory, are the three disciples.

In the "Nativity" the divine Child is on the ground, and around, under a canopy raised on six columns, are kneeling the Madonna, St. Joseph, and the shepherds. There are cattle nearby, and above, in the heavens, three angels singing, and above their heads the words: GLORIA IN EXCELSIS DEO.

On the right wall is a Group of Prophets and Sibyls, Isaiah, Moses, Daniel, David, and Jeremiah, and opposite to them the Persian, Cumæan, Libyan, Tyburtine, and Delphic sibyls. Above them, in the clouds, surrounded by cherubs and adoring angels, is a representation of The Eternal Father.

Near the door is a fine standing figure of Cato, and in the ceiling are medallions of the deities representing the seven planets set amidst a profusion of diversified arabesques.

There are studies in the Uffizi for several of the figures in the Cambio: Socrates (251, 415), Pericles (252, 400), "Moses" (252, 401), "The Cumean Sibyl" (256, 309), "Venus and Cupid" (253, 402), "The Infant Christ" (*verso* of, 252, 401).

ROME, VATICAN, CAPPELLA SISTINA.

St. Peter receiving the Keys.

There is a study in the Uffizi, 252, 416, for one of the heads in this fresco.

ROME, VATICAN, STANZA DELL' INCENDIO.

The CEILING painted by Perugino was spared by Raphael in 1508 when Pope Julius II. ordered the destruction of all existing work in order that Raphael might entirely complete the decoration. The ceiling is in four circular compartments.

The first represents, within a mandorla of cherubs, and surrounded with angels the Eternal Father holding the globe and giving benediction.

The second, the Saviour in glory, within a mandorla, and surrounded with angels and cherubs.

The third, the Saviour surrounded by His apostles and St. Paul, while above Him is the Eternal Father with angels, and at His feet the Dove of the Holy Ghost.

The fourth depicts the Eternal Father between two saints and surrounded by angels and cherubs.

ROME, VATICAN, PINACOTECA.

The Resurrection. Panel. 2·27 x 1·67 = 7 ft. 6 in. x 5 ft. 6 in.

The Madonna and Child. 0·89 x 1·65 = 2 ft. 11 in. x 5 ft. 6 in.

The Virgin is seated on a magnificent canopied throne beneath a vaulted archway. The divine Child is nude, and stands erect on her knees. Around are four saints patrons of Perugia, St. Herculanus, St. Constantius, St. Lawrence, and St. Louis of Toulouse, all richly dressed.

The throne is inscribed: HOC PETRVS DE CHASTRO PLEBIS PINXIT

This was originally in the chapel of the Town Hall at Perugia, for which it was painted, and was carried to Paris in 1797.

SS. Placido, Flavia, and Benedict. 0·31 x 0·26 each.

San Placido bears the Palm, San Benedetto the holy water, asperge, and a book, and Santa Flavia is crowned and has her hands clasped. She and San Placido were brother and sister and early disciples of St. Benedict.

From the pilasters forming the sides of the "Ascension" removed from the Benedictine Church of S. Pietro in Perugia and now at Lyons.

ROME, VILLA BORGHESE.

St. Sebastian. 1·09 x 0·69 = 3 ft. 7 in. x 2 ft. 3 in. [386.]

The saint stands under an open archway, bound to a central column. He is pierced with five arrows, and is looking upwards.

Virgin and Child. 0·45 x 0·37 = 1 ft. 6 in. x 1 ft. 2 in. [401.]
The Virgin is seated, and holds the divine Child, who is nude, erect on her knees.
See Frankfort.

ROME, VILLA ALBANI.

Altar-piece. [37.]
This is in six compartments representing the "Adoration of the Divine Child," and "The Crucifixion." "The Nativity" is below. At the sides are an angel and an Annunciation.
The picture is inscribed on the capitals, PETRVS DE PERVSIA PINXIT MCCVIIII PRIMO.

SIENA, CHURCH OF ST. AGOSTINO.

The Crucifixion.
For this picture Perugino was paid 200 golden ducats.

SINIGAGLIA, MONASTERY CHURCH OF STA. MARIA DELLA GRAZIE.

Virgin and Child with Saints.
The Virgin is on a throne, bearing the divine Child in her arms. Around stand St. John Baptist, St. Louis of France, St. Francis, St. Peter, St. Paul, and St. James (or St. John and St. Andrew).
Almost a replica of the one at Fano.

SPELLO, CHURCH OF SANTA MARIA MAGGIORE.

Pietà.
Our Lady is seated on a throne, and holds the dead body of the Christ in her arms and on her knees. On one side of her kneels Mary Magdalen, and on the right St. John. Above their heads are cherub faces floating in the air. From the canopy of the throne are suspended two tablets bearing these words: PETRVS DE CHASTRO PLEB PINSIT AD MDXXI.; and on the foot of the throne is inscribed: MICHAL AGELVS ANDINE.

Virgin and Child and Saints.

The Virgin is seated on a throne, holding the divine Child, who stands erect and nude on her knees. On her left stands St. Catherine, with wheel and palm, and on the right St. Blaise, in episcopal habit, with mitre and crozier, holding the wool comb.

The throne is inscribed: EX SPEIS JOANNE BERNAR DELLI AD MDXXI DIE XXV APRILIS.

TREVI, CHURCH OF SANTA MARIA DELLE LACRIME.

The Adoration of the Magi.

The throne is inscribed: PETRVS IN CASTRO PLEBIS PINXIT.

TU SOLA IN TERRIS GENETRIX ET VIRGO FVISTIREGINA IN CELIS TV QVOQVE SOLA MANES.

VERONA, MUSEO CIVICO.

The Madonna adoring the Christ. [120.]

The Virgin is standing in the centre of the picture with clasped hands and in front of a stone balustrade. On either side are kneeling angels. The one on the right holds the divine Child, whom the Virgin is adoring, the other rests her hands on the shoulders of St. John Baptist, who is also adoring the Christ. In the background is the usual landscape which appears to be undoubtedly the work of Perugino, and probably also the figure of the Virgin; but the angels and children are school work.

The Adoration of the Magi. [95.]

CHRONOLOGICAL LIST
OF PICTURES

1475

Certain frescoes in the great hall of the Palazzo Publico. Mentioned by Milanesi.

1478

Certain frescoes in a chapel at Cerqueto, a castle in the diocese of Perugia. Also mentioned by Milanesi.

1480

"Christ delivering the keys to St. Peter" in the Sistine Chapel in the Vatican at Rome. Other frescoes now destroyed.

1491

Altar-piece in the Villa Albani. Dated

Rome

1493

Virgin and Child, from Fiesole. Dated

Uffizi, No. 1122

Madonna and Saints. Dated

Vienna

Pietà painted for the Gesuati

Accademia, 58

1494

Madonna and Child. Dated

Sant' Agostino, Cremona

Portrait of Francesco
Uffizi, 287
1495
Madonna and Child
Pinacoteca, Vatican
The Entombment. Dated.
Pitti, 164
The Ascension for San Pietro, Perugia
Centre at Lyons
(A part is dated.)
Predella at Rouen
Other parts at
St. Pietro and the Vatican
1496
Vision of S. Bernardo
Munich
Crucifixion, begun in 1493, finished 1496
Sta. Maria Maddalena dei Pazzi
Virgin and Child at Bologna
Family of Sta. Anna
Marseilles
1497
Altar-piece. Dated
Fano
Virgin and Child. Dated
Pinacoteca, Perugia, Sala xi. 6
1498
Madonna with St. Bernard and St. Francis
Pinacoteca, Perugia, xi. 14
Altar-piece. Dated
Fano
1499-1500
The frescoes in the Cambio
Perugia
Two Monks in the Accademia

17 and 17 bis
A Duke of Urbino
Vienna
1500
The Assumption. Dated
Accademia, 55
1502
Coronation of the Virgin
Pinacoteca, Perugia, Sala viii. 24
1504
Adoration of the Magi. Dated
Città della Pieve
1505
St. Sebastian. Dated
Panicale
Descent from the Cross, begun by Lippi
Accademia, 57
1504 or 5
Love and Chastity
The Louvre, 1567
Virgin and Child with two Saints
Munich, 1035
1507
Virgin and Child with two Saints
National Gallery, 1075
Ceiling in the Camera dell' Incendio
Vatican, Rome
1510
Picture for San Francesco, Siena.
Hertz Coll., Rome
Fragment now remains
Crucifixion. San Agostino
Siena
1512
Votive picture. Dated

Bettona

1513

Virgin in Glory. Dated

Città della Pieve

1517

Descent from the Cross. A fragment. Dated

Città della Pieve

1518

Martyrdom of St. Sebastian. Dated

Pinacoteca, Perugia, Sala x. 2

1521

Additions made to Raphael's unfinished fresco. Dated

S. Severo, Perugia

Pietà. Dated

Spello

Virgin and Child with Saints. Dated

Spello

The Altar-Piece painted for St. Agostino of Perugia, of which part is *in situ*, and other parts are at Lyons, Toulouse, Grenoble, and Nantes

Adoration of the Magi

Trevi

1522

Virgin and Saints. Dated

St. Agnese, Perugia

1523

The Adoration of the Shepherds

National Gallery, 1441

FOOTNOTES

[A] Mariotti, "Lettere Pittoriche Perugine," 1788, v. 121.

[B] "Storia della Pittura," A. Lupattelli. Foligno, 1895.

[C] "Italian Painters," ii. 107.

[D] Eastlake, however, refers to a picture painted for Luca degli' Albizzi for which the artist was paid 100 gold crowns. At this time, it was, he says, in the Palazzo Albizzi, and he says it was executed prior to 1478, as in that year Luca, who was in the Pozzi conspiracy, was exiled for twenty-five years. This picture cannot now be traced.

[E] "Central Italian Painters of the Renaissance," 96.

[F] Mariotti, p. 150.

[G] In 1491 the incomplete picture begun by Galeotto turned up. It had been at his father's house, and quite overlooked; but in that year the heirs of Galeotto's father found it and sent it to the Priori, together with a number of colours that had been prepared for it. For three years the incomplete picture stood in the Priori's room, silently reminding them of Galeotto; but no further progress in the negotiation was made till 1495.

[H] *Magazine of Art,* April 1899.

[I] "The Book of the Art of Cennino Cennini" (Geo. Allen), 1889.

[J] "The Pigments and Vehicles of the Old Masters." Society of Arts, 1892.

[K] *Vide* Gaye ii. 69; and Morelli [1883], 287.

[L] Orsini, "Vita dell' egregio pittore Pietro Perugino," 1804, 140.

[M] Murray, 1899, 253.

[N] In this same year 1510, Perugino painted a "Virgin and Child between St. Peter and St. Paul," for Agostino Spinola of Savona, Bishop of Perugia.

[O] A letter dated 30th March 1512, and written from Città della Pieve, already mentioned, is in existence, and proves not only his presence in the town in that year but that the St. Agostino altar-piece was at that time in hand, although not finished till 1521.

BIBLIOGRAPHY

Austin, Alfred. "Notes made in Perugia." (An article.)

Bell, N. "Tourists' Art Guide to Europe." London, 1893.

Bonacci Brunamonti. "Pietro Perugino" in "Rivista Contemperanea," i. 1889. Fasc. 2.

Brachirolli. "Notizie e documenti inediti intorno a Pietro Vannucci." Perugia, 1874.

Burckhardt. "Art Guide to Painting in Italy." London, 1879.

Bryan. "Dictionary of Painters." London, 1893.

Berenson, B. "Central Italian Painters." London, 1897.

Broussolle, J. C. "Pèlerinages Ombriens." Paris, 1896.

Cennino Cennini. "Trattato della Pittura." Italian, sixteenth century.

"Cennino Cennini, The Book of the Art of." Translated by Mrs. Herringham. London, 1899.

Crowe and Cavalcaselle. "Renaissance in Italy." London, 1877.

Church, A. H. "Cantor Lectures on Colours." London, 1890.

Eastlake, Sir C. "History of Painting."

Gaye. "Carteggio."

Galetti, G. "Lo Stile di Pietro Perugino e l'indirizzo dell' Arte Moderna." Bologna, 1887.

"Gazette des Beaux Arts."

Hare, A. "Cities of Central Italy." London, 1876.

Heaton, Mrs. "History of Painting." London, 1873.

Hoefer. "Bibliographical Dictionary." Paris, 1860 xiv].

Jameson, Mrs. All her works. London, 1872.

Kugler. "Handbook of Painting." London, 1855.

Lanzi, Luigi. "Storia Pittorica della Italia." Bassano, 1809.

Lomazzo. "Idea del tempio della Pittura." Rome, 1844.

Lafenestre. "Les Maitres anciens." 1882.

Lafenestre. "La Peinture Italienne."

Lafenestre and Richtenburger. "The Louvre." Paris, 1898.

Luebke, W. "History of Art." London, 1868.

Laurie, A. P. "Cantor Lectures on Vehicles and Pigments." London, 1892.

Lupattelli, A. "Storia della Pittura in Perugia." Foligno, 1895.

Lupattelli, A. "Petit Guide de Pérouse." Paris, 1895.

Lee, Vernon. "In Umbria." (Articles.)

Muntz, E. "Raphael." Translated by Armstrong. London, 1882.

Muntz, M. "La fin de la Renaissance."

Marchesi. "Il Cambio di Perugia." Prato, 1853.

Mezzanotte. "Della vita e delle opere di Pietro Vannucci." Perugia, 1836.

Morelli. "Italian Painters in German Galleries." London, 1882.

Morelli. "Italian Painters," Vols. i. and ii. London, 1892-3.

Morelli. "Della Pittura Italiana." Milan, 1897.

Mariotti. "Lettere Pittoriche Perugine." 1788.

Orsini. "Vita e Elegio dell' egregio pittore Perugino e degli Scolari di esso." Perugia, 1804.

Pascoli. "Vite de Pittori Perugini."

Passavant, J. D. "Raphael d' Urbin e xv]t son père." Appendix, 445-461. "Essai sur les Peintres de l'Ombrie." Paris, 1860.

Poynter, Sir E. J. "Classical and Italian Painting." 1897.

Phillips, Claud. "Perugino" in the "Portfolio." London, 1893.

Rio, A. F. "De l'Art Chrétien." Paris, 1874.

Ris, Clement De. "Les Musées de Province de France."

Rosini. "Storia della Pittura Italiana." Pisa, 1847.

Rumohr. "Italienische Forschungen," ii.

Rossi, A. "Storia artistica del Cambio di Perugia." Perugia, 1874.

Rossi-Scotti. "Guida Illustrata di Perugia." Perugia, 1878.

Rea, Hope. "Tuscan Artists." London, 1898.

Symonds and Gordon. "Story of Perugia." London, 1898.

Symonds, J. A. "Italian Byeways."

Symonds, J. A. "Sketches and Studies in Southern Europe."

Symonds, J. A. "Renaissance in Italy." London, 1877.

Vasari, G. "Delle Vite de piu Eccelenti Pittori." Firenze, 1550

Vasari, G. Mrs Foster's Translation. London, 1894.

Vasari, G. Blashfield and Hopkin's Edition. London, 1897.

Vermiglioli. "Memorie di Ber. Pinturicchio."

Viardot. "Les Merveilles de la Peinture." Paris, 1870.

Woltman and Woerman. "History of Painting." 1880.

Yriarte, C. "Isabella d'Este et les artistes de son temps."

CRESCENT MOON PUBLISHING

web: www.crmoon.com e-mail: cresmopub@yahoo.co.uk

ARTS, PAINTING, SCULPTURE

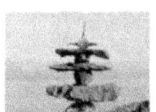
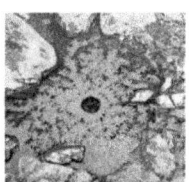
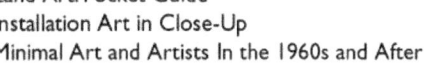

The Art of Andy Goldsworthy
Andy Goldsworthy: Touching Nature
Andy Goldsworthy in Close-Up
Andy Goldsworthy: Pocket Guide
Andy Goldsworthy In America
Land Art: A Complete Guide
The Art of Richard Long
Richard Long: Pocket Guide
Land Art In the UK
Land Art in Close-Up
Land Art In the U.S.A.
Land Art: Pocket Guide
Installation Art in Close-Up
Minimal Art and Artists In the 1960s and After
Colourfield Painting
Land Art DVD, TV documentary
Andy Goldsworthy DVD, TV documentary
The Erotic Object: Sexuality in Sculpture From Prehistory to the Present Day
Sex in Art: Pornography and Pleasure in Painting and Sculpture
Postwar Art
Sacred Gardens: The Garden in Myth, Religion and Art
Glorification: Religious Abstraction in Renaissance and 20th Century Art
Early Netherlandish Painting
Leonardo da Vinci
Piero della Francesca
Giovanni Bellini
Fra Angelico: Art and Religion in the Renaissance
Mark Rothko: The Art of Transcendence
Frank Stella: American Abstract Artist
Jasper Johns
Brice Marden
Alison Wilding: The Embrace of Sculpture
Vincent van Gogh: Visionary Landscapes
Eric Gill: Nuptials of God
Constantin Brancusi: Sculpting the Essence of Things
Max Beckmann
Caravaggio
Gustave Moreau
Egon Schiele: Sex and Death In Purple Stockings
Delizioso Fotografico Fervore: Works In Process 1
Sacro Cuore: Works In Process 2
The Light Eternal: J.M.W. Turner
The Madonna Glorified: Karen Arthurs

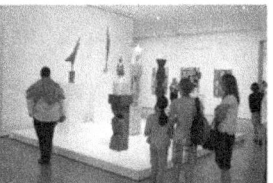
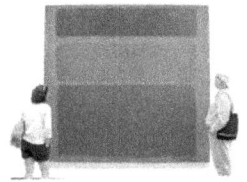
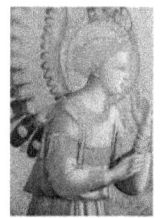
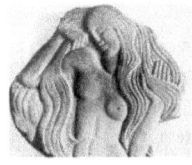
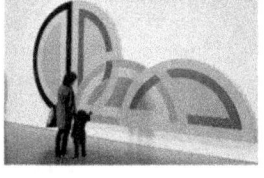
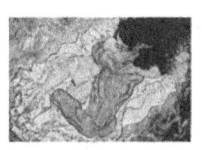
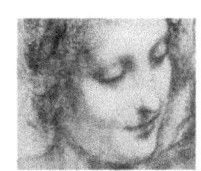
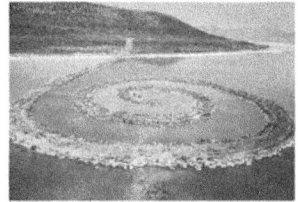

LITERATURE

J.R.R. Tolkien: The Books, The Films, The Whole Cultural Phenomenon
J.R.R. Tolkien: Pocket Guide
Tolkien's Heroic Quest
The *Earthsea* Books of Ursula Le Guin
Beauties, Beasts and Enchantment: Classic French Fairy Tales
German Popular Stories by the Brothers Grimm
Philip Pullman and *His Dark Materials*
Sexing Hardy: Thomas Hardy and Feminism
Thomas Hardy's *Tess of the d'Urbervilles*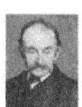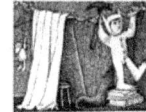
Thomas Hardy's *Jude the Obscure*
Thomas Hardy: The Tragic Novels
Love and Tragedy: Thomas Hardy
The Poetry of Landscape in Hardy
Wessex Revisited: Thomas Hardy and John Cowper Powys
Wolfgang Iser: Essays and Interviews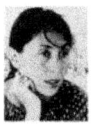
Petrarch, Dante and the Troubadours
Maurice Sendak and the Art of Children's Book Illustration
Andrea Dworkin
Cixous, Irigaray, Kristeva: The *Jouissance* of French Feminism
Julia Kristeva: Art, Love, Melancholy, Philosophy, Semiotics and Psychoanalysis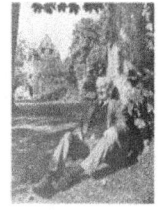
Hélène Cixous I Love You: The *Jouissance* of Writing
Luce Irigaray: Lips, Kissing, and the Politics of Sexual Difference
Peter Redgrove: Here Comes the Flood
Peter Redgrove: Sex-Magic-Poetry-Cornwall
Lawrence Durrell: Between Love and Death, East and West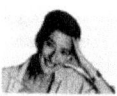
Love, Culture & Poetry: Lawrence Durrell
Cavafy: Anatomy of a Soul
German Romantic Poetry: Goethe, Novalis, Heine, Hölderlin
Feminism and Shakespeare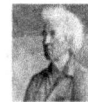
Shakespeare: Love, Poetry & Magic
The Passion of D.H. Lawrence
D.H. Lawrence: Symbolic Landscapes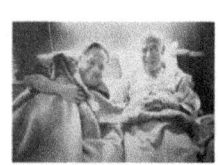
D.H. Lawrence: Infinite Sensual Violence
Rimbaud: Arthur Rimbaud and the Magic of Poetry
The Ecstasies of John Cowper Powys
Sensualism and Mythology: The Wessex Novels of John Cowper Powys
Amorous Life: John Cowper Powys and the Manifestation of Affectivity (H.W. Fawkner)
Postmodern Powys: New Essays on John Cowper Powys (Joe Boulter)
Rethinking Powys: Critical Essays on John Cowper Powys
Paul Bowles & Bernardo Bertolucci
Rainer Maria Rilke
Joseph Conrad: *Heart of Darkness*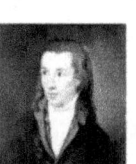
In the Dim Void: Samuel Beckett
Samuel Beckett Goes into the Silence
André Gide: Fiction and Fervour
Jackie Collins and the Blockbuster Novel
Blinded By Her Light: The Love-Poetry of Robert Graves
The Passion of Colours: Travels In Mediterranean Lands
Poetic Forms

POETRY

Ursula Le Guin: Walking In Cornwall
Peter Redgrove: Here Comes The Flood
Peter Redgrove: Sex-Magic-Poetry-Cornwall
Dante: Selections From the Vita Nuova
Petrarch, Dante and the Troubadours
William Shakespeare: Sonnets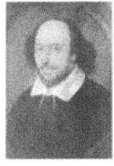
William Shakespeare: Complete Poems
Blinded By Her Light: The Love-Poetry of Robert Graves
Emily Dickinson: Selected Poems
Emily Brontë: Poems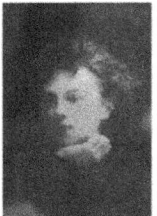
Thomas Hardy: Selected Poems
Percy Bysshe Shelley: Poems
John Keats: Selected Poems
Joh n Keats: Poems of 1820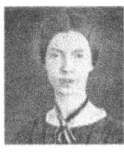
D.H. Lawrence: Selected Poems
Edmund Spenser: Poems
Edmund Spenser: Amoretti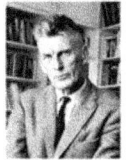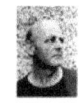
John Donne: Poems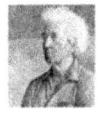
Henry Vaughan: Poems
Sir Thomas Wyatt: Poems
Robert Herrick: Selected Poems
Rilke: Space, Essence and Angels in the Poetry of Rainer Maria Rilke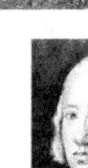
Rainer Maria Rilke: Selected Poems
Friedrich Hölderlin: Selected Poems
Arseny Tarkovsky: Selected Poems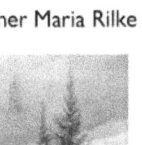
Arthur Rimbaud: Selected Poems
Arthur Rimbaud: A Season in Hell
Arthur Rimbaud and the Magic of Poetry
Novalis: Hymns To the Night
German Romantic Poetry
Paul Verlaine: Selected Poems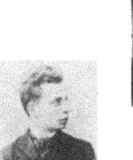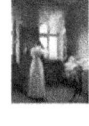
Elizaethan Sonnet Cycles
D.J. Enright: By-Blows
Jeremy Reed: Brigitte's Blue Heart
Jeremy Reed: Claudia Schiffer's Red Shoes
Gorgeous Little Orpheus
Radiance: New Poems
Crescent Moon Book of Nature Poetry
Crescent Moon Book of Love Poetry
Crescent Moon Book of Mystical Poetry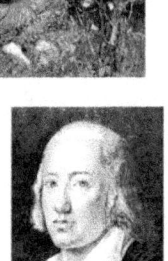
Crescent Moon Book of Elizabethan Love Poetry
Crescent Moon Book of Metaphysical Poetry
Crescent Moon Book of Romantic Poetry
Pagan America: New American Poetry

MEDIA, CINEMA, FEMINISM and CULTURAL STUDIES

J.R.R. Tolkien: The Books, The Films, The Whole Cultural Phenomenon
J.R.R. Tolkien: Pocket Guide
The *Lord of the Rings* Movies: Pocket Guide
The Cinema of Hayao Miyazaki
Hayao Miyazaki: *Princess Mononoke*: Pocket Movie Guide
Hayao Miyazaki: *Spirited Away*: Pocket Movie Guide
Tim Burton : Hallowe'en For Hollywood
Ken Russell
Ken Russell: *Tommy*: Pocket Movie Guide
The Ghost Dance: The Origins of Religion
The Peyote Cult
Cixous, Irigaray, Kristeva: The *Jouissance* of French Feminism
Julia Kristeva: Art, Love, Melancholy, Philosophy, Semiotics and Psychoanalysis
Luce Irigaray: Lips, Kissing, and the Politics of Sexual Difference
Hélene Cixous I Love You: The *Jouissance* of Writing
Andrea Dworkin
'Cosmo Woman': The World of Women's Magazines
Women in Pop Music
HomeGround: The Kate Bush Anthology
Discovering the Goddess (Geoffrey Ashe)
The Poetry of Cinema
The Sacred Cinema of Andrei Tarkovsky
Andrei Tarkovsky: Pocket Guide
Andrei Tarkovsky: *Mirror*: Pocket Movie Guide
Andrei Tarkovsky: *The Sacrifice*: Pocket Movie Guide
Walerian Borowczyk: Cinema of Erotic Dreams
Jean-Luc Godard: The Passion of Cinema
Jean-Luc Godard: *Hail Mary*: Pocket Movie Guide
Jean-Luc Godard: *Contempt*: Pocket Movie Guide
Jean-Luc Godard: *Pierrot le Fou*: Pocket Movie Guide
John Hughes and Eighties Cinema
Ferris Bueller's Day Off: Pocket Movie Guide
Jean-Luc Godard: Pocket Guide
The Cinema of Richard Linklater
Liv Tyler: Star In Ascendance
Blade Runner and the Films of Philip K. Dick
Paul Bowles and Bernardo Bertolucci
Media Hell: Radio, TV and the Press
An Open Letter to the BBC
Detonation Britain: Nuclear War in the UK
Feminism and Shakespeare
Wild Zones: Pornography, Art and Feminism
Sex in Art: Pornography and Pleasure in Painting and Sculpture
Sexing Hardy: Thomas Hardy and Feminism

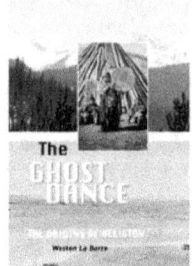
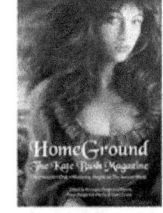
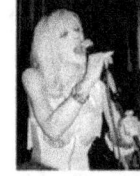
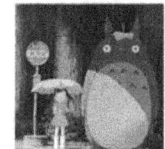
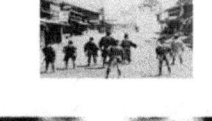

The Light Eternal is a model monograph, an exemplary job. The subject matter of the book is beautifully
organised and dead on beam. (Lawrence Durrell)
It is amazing for me to see my work treated with such passion and respect. (Andrea Dworkin)

CRESCENT MOON PUBLISHING
P.O. Box 1312, Maidstone, Kent, ME14 5XU, Great Britain. www.crmoon.com

cresmopub@yahoo.co.uk   www.crescentmoon.org.uk

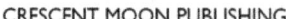